MongoDB Basics

David Hows
Peter Membrey
Eelco Plugge

Apress®

MongoDB Basics

ISBN-13 (pbk): 978-1-4842-0896-0

ISBN-13 (electronic): 978-1-4842-0895-3

Managing Director: Welmoed Spahr
Lead Editor: Michelle Lowman
Development Editor: Douglas Pundick
Technical Reviewers: Alexandre Beaulne and Stephen Steneker
Editorial Board: Steve Anglin, Mark Beckner, Gary Cornell, Louise Corrigan, Jim DeWolf,
    Jonathan Gennick, Robert Hutchinson, Michelle Lowman, James Markham,
    Matthew Moodie, Jeff Olson, Jeffrey Pepper, Douglas Pundick, Ben Renow-Clarke,
    Gwenan Spearing, Matt Wade, Steve Weiss
Coordinating Editor: Kevin Walter
Compositor: SPi Global
Indexer: SPi Global
Artist: SPi Global
Cover Designer: Anna Ishchenko

Distributed to the book trade worldwide by Springer Science+Business Media New York, 233 Spring Street, 6th Floor, New York, NY 10013. Phone 1-800-SPRINGER, fax (201) 348-4505, e-mail orders-ny@springer-sbm.com, or visit www.springeronline.com. Apress Media, LLC is a California LLC and the sole member (owner) is Springer Science + Business Media Finance Inc (SSBM Finance Inc). SSBM Finance Inc is a **Delaware** corporation.

For information on translations, please e-mail rights@apress.com, or visit www.apress.com.

Apress and friends of ED books may be purchased in bulk for academic, corporate, or promotional use. eBook versions and licenses are also available for most titles. For more information, reference our Special Bulk Sales–eBook Licensing web page at www.apress.com/bulk-sales.

Any source code or other supplementary material referenced by the author in this text is available to readers at www.apress.com. For detailed information about how to locate your book's source code, go to www.apress.com/source-code/.

We would all like to dedicate this book to the same person, someone who only one of us has ever actually met but someone who has had a significant impact on all of our lives. 15 years ago Dave Uden took something of a risk to support one of us and helped us achieve our potential. That support changed everything and profoundly affected how that person saw the world. In the coming years, that person extended the same support openly to others, two of whom he now considers two of his closest friends. All of us feel that our lives would have been very different without that initial support.

To Dave Uden, then, we extend our sincerest thanks. We owe you more than words can say.

Contents at a Glance

Contents

About the Authors

David Hows is an Honors graduate from the University of Woolongong in NSW, Australia. He got his start in computing trying to drive more performance out of his family PC without spending a fortune. This led to a career in IT, where David has worked as a Systems Administrator, Performance Engineer, Software Developer, Solutions Architect, and Database Engineer. David has tried in vain for many years to play soccer well, and his coffee mug reads "Grumble Bum."

Peter Membrey is a Chartered IT Fellow with nearly 15 years of experience using Linux and open source solutions to solve problems in the real world. An RHCE since the age of 17, he has also had the honor of working for Red Hat and writing several books covering open source solutions. He holds a master's degree in IT (Information Security) from the University of Liverpool and is currently an EngD candidate at the Hong Kong Polytechnic University, where his research interests include cloud computing, big data, science, and security. He lives in Hong Kong with his wonderful wife Sarah and son Kaydyn. His Cantonese continues to regress, though his Esperanto is coming along nicely.

Eelco Plugge is a young IET/BSC Professional showing a great interest in the field of IT security. He started working as an encryption specialist at the tender age of 21, and is currently involved in the Mobile Device Management industry while sporadically writing a book. Eelco has recently completed his MSc in Computer Security at the University of Liverpool, holds several professional certifications, and has a passion for Linux, network security, and encryption technologies. Eelco lives in the Netherlands with his young family. Loves sushi, hates overcomplicating matters.

About the Technical Reviewers

Originally from Canada's great north, **Alexandre Beaulne** pursued a bachelor degree in systems neuroscience at McGill University in Montreal, followed by a master's degree in financial engineering at HEC Montreal. His studies, however, culminated in his attendance at Hacker School in New York City. He has repeatedly made the unsupported claim that he "gets" Haskell's monads.

Stephen Steneker (aka Stennie) is an experienced full stack software developer, consultant, and instructor. Stephen has a long history working for Australian technology startups including founding technical roles at Yahoo! Australia & NZ, HomeScreen Entertainment, and Grox. He holds a BSc (Computer Science) from the University of British Columbia.

In his current role as a Technical Services Engineer for MongoDB, Inc., Stephen provides support, consulting, and training for MongoDB. He frequently speaks at user groups and conferences, and is the founder and wrangler for the Sydney MongoDB User Group (http://www.meetup.com/SydneyMUG/).

You can find him on Twitter, StackOverflow, or Github as @stennie.

Acknowledgments

My thanks to all members of the MongoDB team, past and present. Without them we would not be here, and the way people think about the storage of data would be radically different. I would like to pay extra special thanks to my colleagues at the MongoDB team in Sydney, as without them I would not be here today.

Lastly, I would like to thank my loving Fiance, Jacqui. For all her love and support throughout.

—David Hows

Writing a book is always a team effort. Even when there is just a single author, there are many people working behind the scenes to pull everything together. With that in mind I want to thank everyone in the MongoDB community and everyone at Apress for all their hard work, patience, and support. Special thanks go to Dave and Eelco for really driving the Second Edition home.

I'd also like to thank Chuck Smith, a friend (and founder of the Esperanto language version of Wikipedia) who got me hooked on Esperanto and kept my motivation nice and high. It coincided with my work on the Second Edition, and I am positive that the excitement from learning Esperanto spilled over into this rewrite. Thanks must also go to Dr. L. L. Zamenhof, the man who created Esperanto. A man way ahead of his time, and I hope to carry that dream forward.

Lastly, thanks to my wife Sarah for being patient and supportive as always.

—Peter Membrey

To the 9gag community, without whom this book would have been finished months ago.

—Eelco Plugge

Introduction

Its a pleasure for me to be able to once again introduce a new audience to MongoDB. Throughout my tenure as a computer engineer, it is one of several technologies that I have had the pleasure of working with in depth. I am cotinually supprised at the number of different configurations and purposes that MongoDB is put to.

We see this book as being a small primer and introduction to MongoDB. In order to have such a wide variety of uses a tool must be infinitely flexible, which MongoDB is. At the same time, this flexibility does come with a small learning curve and that is why this book exists. We aim to provide people with a great way to look at many of the core storage features of MongoDB. To do this, we have eschewed some of the more complex operational features such as Sharding and Replication, we also avoided going into depth with a lot of the operations level mechanics.

With all this in mind, we hope that you find this book to be a great way to build your apetite for one of the most disruptive technologies of the 21st century! Good luck and enjoy.

CHAPTER 1

■ ■ ■

Introduction to MongoDB

Imagine a world where using a database is so simple that you soon forget you're even using it. Imagine a world where speed and scalability *just work*, and there's no need for complicated configuration or setup. Imagine being able to focus only on the task at hand, get things done, and then—just for a change—leave work on time. That might sound a bit fanciful, but MongoDB promises to help you accomplish all these things (and more).

MongoDB (derived from the word *humongous*) is a relatively new breed of database that has no concept of tables, schemas, SQL, or rows. It doesn't have transactions, ACID compliance, joins, foreign keys, or many of the other features that tend to cause headaches in the early hours of the morning. In short, MongoDB is a very different database than you're probably used to, especially if you've used a relational database management system (RDBMS) in the past. In fact, you might even be shaking your head in wonder at the lack of so-called "standard" features.

Fear not! In the following pages, you will learn about MongoDB's background and guiding principles, and why the MongoDB team made the design decisions that it did. We'll also take a whistle-stop tour of MongoDB's feature list, providing just enough detail to ensure that you'll be completely hooked on this topic for the rest of the book.

We'll start by looking at the philosophy and ideas behind the creation of MongoDB, as well as some of the interesting and somewhat controversial design decisions. We'll explore the concept of document-oriented databases, how they fit together, and what their strengths and weaknesses are. We'll also explore JSON and examine how it applies to MongoDB. To wrap things up, we'll step through some of the notable features of MongoDB.

Reviewing the MongoDB Philosophy

Like all projects, MongoDB has a set of design philosophies that help guide its development. In this section, we'll review some of the database's founding principles.

Using the Right Tool for the Right Job

The most important of the philosophies that underpin MongoDB is the notion that *one size does not fit all*. For many years, traditional relational (SQL) databases (MongoDB is a document-oriented database) have been used for storing content of all types. It didn't matter whether the data was a good fit for the relational model (which is used in all RDBMS databases, such as MySQL, PostgresSQL, SQLite, Oracle, MS SQL Server, and

1

so on); the data was stuffed in there, anyway. Part of the reason for this is that, generally speaking, it's much easier (and more secure) to read and write to a database than it is to write to a file system. If you pick up any book that teaches PHP, such as *PHP for Absolute Beginners,* by Jason Lengstorf (Apress, 2009), you'll probably find that almost right away the database is used to store information, not the file system. It's just so much easier to do things that way. And while using a database as a storage bin works, developers always have to work against the flow. It's usually obvious when we're not using the database the way it was intended; anyone who has ever tried to store information with even slightly complex data, had to set up five tables, and then tried to pull it all together knows what we're talking about!

The MongoDB team decided that it wasn't going to create another database that tries to do everything for everyone. Instead, the team wanted to create a database that worked with documents rather than rows and that was blindingly fast, massively scalable, and easy to use. To do this, the team had to leave some features behind, which means that MongoDB is not an ideal candidate for certain situations. For example, its lack of transaction support means that you wouldn't want to use MongoDB to write an accounting application. That said, MongoDB might be perfect for part of the aforementioned application (such as storing complex data). That's not a problem, though, because there is no reason why you can't use a traditional RDBMS for the accounting components and MongoDB for the document storage. Such hybrid solutions are quite common, and you can see them in production apps such as the New York Times website.

Once you're comfortable with the idea that MongoDB may not solve all your problems, you will discover that there are certain problems that MongoDB is a perfect fit for resolving, such as analytics (think a real-time Google Analytics for your website) and complex data structures (for example, blog posts and comments). If you're still not convinced that MongoDB is a serious database tool, feel free to skip ahead to the "Reviewing the Feature List" section, where you will find an impressive list of features for MongoDB.

■ **Note** The lack of transactions and other traditional database features doesn't mean that MongoDB is unstable or that it cannot be used for managing important data.

Another key concept behind MongoDB's design is that there should always be more than one copy of the database. If a single database should fail, then it can simply be restored from the other servers. Because MongoDB aims to be as fast as possible, it takes some shortcuts that make it more difficult to recover from a crash. The developers believe that most serious crashes are likely to remove an entire computer from service anyway; this means that even if the database were perfectly restored, it would still not be usable. Remember: MongoDB does not try to be everything to everyone. But for many purposes (such as building a web application), MongoDB can be an awesome tool for implementing your solution.

So now you know where MongoDB is coming from. It's not trying to be the best at everything, and it readily acknowledges that it's not for everyone. However, for those who do choose to use it, MongoDB provides a rich document-oriented database that's optimized for speed and scalability. It can also run nearly anywhere you might want to run it. MongoDB's website includes downloads for Linux, Mac OS, Windows, and Solaris.

MongoDB succeeds at all these goals, and this is why using MongoDB (at least for us) is somewhat dream-like. You don't have to worry about squeezing your data into a table—just put the data together, and then pass it to MongoDB for handling.Consider this real-world example. A recent application co-author Peter Membrey worked on needed to store a set of eBay search results. There could be any number of results (up to 100 of them), and he needed an easy way to associate the results with the users in his database.

Had Peter been using MySQL, he would have had to design a table to store the data, write the code to store his results, and then write more code to piece it all back together again. This is a fairly common scenario and one most developers face on a regular basis. Normally, we just get on with it; however, for this project, he was using MongoDB, and so things went a bit differently.

Specifically, he added this line of code:

```
request['ebay_results'] = ebay_results_array
collection.save(request)
```

In this example, `request` is Peter's document, `ebay_results` is the key, and `ebay_result_array` contains the results from eBay. The second line saves the changes. When he accesses this document in the future, he will have the eBay results in exactly the same format as before. He doesn't need any SQL; he doesn't need to perform any conversions; nor does he need to create any new tables or write any special code—MongoDB just worked. It got out of the way, he finished his work early, and he got to go home on time.

Lacking Innate Support for Transactions

Here's another important design decision by MongoDB developers: The database does not include transactional semantics (the element that offers guarantees about data consistency and storage). This is a solid tradeoff based on MongoDB's goal of being simple, fast, and scalable. Once you leave those heavyweight features at the door, it becomes much easier to scale horizontally.

Normally with a traditional RDBMS, you improve performance by buying a bigger, more powerful machine. This is scaling vertically, but you can only take it so far. With horizontal scaling, rather than having one big machine, you have lots of less powerful small machines. Historically, clusters of servers like this were excellent for load-balancing websites, but databases had always been a problem because of internal design limitations.

You might think this missing support constitutes a deal-breaker; however, many people forget that one of the most popular table types in MySQL (`MYISAM`—which also happens to be the default) doesn't support transactions, either. This fact hasn't stopped MySQL from becoming and remaining the dominant open source database for well over a decade. As with most choices when developing solutions, using MongoDB is going to be a matter of personal preference and whether the tradeoffs fit your project.

■ **Note**   MongoDB offers durability when used in tandem with at least three servers, which is the recommended minimum for production deployments. It is possible to make the primary replica member wait for one or more of the secondary members to confirm receipt of the data before the primary itself confirms that the data has been accepted.

JSON and MongoDB

JSON (Java Script Object Notation) is more than a great way to exchange data; it's also a nice way to store data. An RDBMS is highly structured, with multiple files (tables) that store the individual pieces. MongoDB, on the other hand, stores everything together in a single document. MongoDB is like JSON in this way, and this model provides a rich and expressive way of storing data. Moreover, JSON effectively describes all the content in a given document, so there is no need to specify the structure of the document in advance. JSON is effectively *schemaless* (that is, it doesn't require a schema), because documents can be updated individually or changed independently of any other documents. As an added bonus, JSON also provides excellent performance by keeping all of the related data in one place.

MongoDB doesn't actually use JSON to store the data; rather, it uses an open data format developed by the MongoDB team called *BSON* (pronounced Bee-Son), which is short for binary JSON. For the most part, using BSON instead of JSON won't change how you work with your data. BSON makes MongoDB even faster by making it much easier for a computer to process and search documents. BSON also adds a couple of features that aren't available in standard JSON, including the ability to add types for handling binary data. We'll look at BSON in more depth in "Using Document-Oriented Storage (BSON)," later in this chapter.

The original specification for JSON can be found in RFC 4627, and it was written by Douglas Crockford. JSON allows complex data structures to be represented in a simple, human-readable text format that is generally considered to be much easier to read and understand than XML. Like XML, JSON was envisaged as a way to exchange data between a web client (such as a browser) and web applications. When combined with the rich way that it can describe objects, its simplicity has made it the exchange format of choice for the majority of developers.

You might wonder what is meant here by *complex data structures*. Historically, data was exchanged using the comma-separated values (CSV) format (indeed, this approach remains very common today). CSV is a simple text format that separates rows with a new line and fields with a comma. For example, a CSV file might look like this:

```
Membrey, Peter, +852 1234 5678
Thielen, Wouter, +81 1234 5678
```

A human can look at this information and see quite quickly what information is being communicated. Or maybe not—is that number in the third column a phone number or a fax number? It might even be the number for a pager. To avoid this ambiguity, CSV files often have a header field, in which the first row defines what comes in the file. The following snippet takes the previous example one step further:

```
Lastname, Firstname, Phone Number
Membrey, Peter, +852 1234 5678
Thielen, Wouter, +81 1234 5678
```

Okay, that's a bit better. But now assume some people in the CSV file have more than one phone number. You could add another field for an office phone number, but you face a new set of issues if you want several office phone numbers. And you face yet another set of issues if you also want to incorporate multiple e-mail addresses. Most people have more than one, and these addresses can't usually be neatly defined as either home or work. Suddenly, CSV starts to show its limitations. CSV files are only good for storing data that is flat and doesn't have repeating values. Similarly, it's not uncommon for several CSV files to be provided, each with the separate bits of information. These files are then combined (usually in an RDBMS) to create the whole picture. As an example, a large retail company may receive sales data in the form of CSV files from each of its stores at the end of each day. These files must be combined before the company can see how it performed on a given day. This process is not exactly straightforward, and it certainly increases chances of a mistake as the number of required files grows.

XML largely solves this problem, but using XML for most things is a bit like using a sledgehammer to crack a nut: it works, but it feels like overkill. The reason for this is that XML is highly extensible. Rather than define a particular data format, XML defines how you define a data format. This can be useful when you need to exchange complex and highly structured data; however, for simple data exchange, it often results in too much work. Indeed, this scenario is the source of the phrase "XML hell."

JSON provides a happy medium. Unlike CSV, it can store structured content; but unlike XML, JSON makes the content easy to understand and simple to use. Let's revisit the previous example; however, this time you will use JSON rather than CSV:

```
{
    "firstname": "Peter",
    "lastname": "Membrey",
    "phone_numbers": [
        "+852 1234 5678",
        "+44 1234 565 555"
    ]
}
```

In this version of the example, each JSON object (or document) contains all the information needed to understand it. If you look at phone_numbers, you can see that it contains a list of different numbers. This list can be as large as you want. You could also be more specific about the type of number being recorded, as in this example:

```
{
    "firstname": "Peter",
    "lastname": "Membrey",
    "numbers": [
        {
            "phone": "+852 1234 5678"
        },
        {
            "fax": "+44 1234 565 555"
        }
    ]
}
```

This version of the example improves on things a bit more. Now you can clearly see what each number is for. JSON is extremely expressive, and, although it's quite easy to write JSON by hand, it is usually generated automatically in software. For example, Python includes a module called (somewhat predictably) json that takes existing Python objects and automatically converts them to JSON. Because JSON is supported and used on so many platforms, it is an ideal choice for exchanging data.

When you add items such as the list of phone numbers, you are actually creating what is known as an *embedded document*. This happens whenever you add complex content such as a list (or *array*, to use the term favored in JSON). Generally speaking, there is also a logical distinction. For example, a Person document might have several Address documents embedded inside it. Similarly, an Invoice document might have numerous LineItem documents embedded inside it. Of course, the embedded Address document could also have its own embedded document that contains phone numbers, for example.

Whether you choose to embed a particular document is determined when you decide how to store your information. This is usually referred to as *schema design*. It might seem odd to refer to schema design when MongoDB is considered a schemaless database. However, while MongoDB doesn't force you to create a schema or enforce one that you create, you do still need to think about how your data fits together. We'll look at this in more depth in Chapter 3.

Adopting a Nonrelational Approach

Improving performance with a relational database is usually straightforward: you buy a bigger, faster server. And this works great until you reach the point where there isn't a bigger server available to buy. At that point, the only option is to spread out to two servers. This might sound easy, but it is a stumbling block for most databases. For example, neither MySQL nor PostgresSQL can run a single database on two servers, where both servers can both read and write data (often referred to as an *active/active cluster*). And although Oracle can do this with its impressive Real Application Clusters (RAC) architecture, you can expect to take out a mortgage if you want to use that solution—implementing a RAC-based solution requires multiple servers, shared storage, and several software licenses.

You might wonder why having an active/active cluster on two databases is so difficult. When you query your database, the database has to find all the relevant data and link it all together. RDBMS solutions feature many ingenious ways to improve performance, but they all rely on having a complete picture of the data available. And this is where you hit a wall: this approach simply doesn't work when half the data is on another server.

Of course, you might have a small database that simply gets lots of requests, so you just need to share the workload. Unfortunately, here you hit another wall. You need to ensure that data written to the first server is available to the second server. And you face additional issues if updates are made on two separate masters simultaneously. For example, you need to determine which update is the correct one. Another problem you can encounter: someone might query the second server for information that has just been written to the first server, but that information hasn't been updated yet on the second server. When you consider all these issues, it becomes easy to see why the Oracle solution is so expensive—these problems are extremely hard to address.

MongoDB solves the active/active cluster problems in a very clever way—it avoids them completely. Recall that MongoDB stores data in BSON documents, so the data is self-contained. That is, although similar documents are stored together, individual documents aren't made up of relationships. This means that everything you need is all in one place. Because queries in MongoDB look for specific keys and values in a document, this information can be easily spread across as many servers as you have available. Each server checks the content it has and returns the result. This effectively allows almost linear scalability and performance. As an added bonus, it doesn't even require that you take out a new mortgage to pay for this functionality.

Admittedly, MongoDB does not offer *master/master replication*, in which two separate servers can both accept write requests. However, it does have *sharding*, which allows data to split across multiple machines, with each machine responsible for updating different parts of the dataset. The benefit of this design is that, while some solutions allow two master databases, MongoDB can potentially scale to hundreds of machines as easily as it can run on two.

Opting for Performance vs. Features

Performance is important, but MongoDB also provides a large feature set. We've already discussed some of the features MongoDB doesn't implement, and you might be somewhat skeptical of the claim that MongoDB achieves its impressive performance partly by judiciously excising certain features common to other databases. However, there are analogous database systems available that are extremely fast, but also extremely limited, such as those that implement a key/value store.

A perfect example is *memcached*. This application was written to provide high-speed data caching, and it is mind-numbingly fast. When used to cache website content, it can speed up an application many times over. This application is used by extremely large websites, such as Facebook and LiveJournal.

The catch is that this application has two significant shortcomings. First, it is a memory-only database. If the power goes out, then all the data is lost. Second, you can't actually search for data using memcached; you can only request specific keys.

These might sound like serious limitations; however, you must remember the problems that memcached is designed to solve. First and foremost, memcached is a data cache. That is, it's not supposed to be a permanent data store, but only to provide a caching layer for your existing database. When you build a dynamic web page, you generally request very specific data (such as the current top ten articles). This means you can specifically ask memcached for that data—there is no need to perform a search. If the cache is out-of-date or empty, you would query your database as normal, build up the data, and then store it in memcached for future use.

Once you accept these limitations, you can see how memcached offers superb performance by implementing a very limited feature set. This performance, by the way, is unmatched by that of a traditional database. That said, memcached certainly can't replace an RDBMS. The important thing to keep in mind is that it's not supposed to.

Compared to memcached, MongoDB is itself feature-rich. To be useful, MongoDB must offer a strong set of features, such as the ability to search for specific documents. It must also be able to store those documents on disk, so that they can survive a reboot. Fortunately, MongoDB provides enough features to be a strong contender for most web applications and many other types of applications as well.

Like memcached, MongoDB is not a one-size-fits-all database. As is usually the case in computing, tradeoffs must be made to achieve the intended goals of the application.

Running the Database Anywhere

MongoDB is written in C++, which makes it relatively easy to port and/or run the application practically anywhere. Currently, binaries can be downloaded from the MongoDB website for Linux, Mac OS, Windows, and Solaris. There are also various official versions available for Fedora and CentOS, among other platforms. You can even download the source code and build your own MongoDB, although it is recommended that you use the provided binaries wherever possible. All the binaries are available in both 32-bit and 64-bit versions.

■ **Caution**   The 32-bit version of MongoDB is limited to databases of 2GB or less. This is because MongoDB uses memory-mapped files internally to achieve high performance. Anything larger than 2GB on a 32-bit system would require some fancy footwork that wouldn't be fast and would also complicate the application's code. The official stance on this limitation is that 64-bit environments are easily available; therefore, increasing code complexity is not a good tradeoff. The 64-bit version for all intents and purposes has no such restriction.

MongoDB's modest requirements allow it to run on high-powered servers or virtual machines, and even to power cloud-based applications. By keeping things simple and focusing on speed and efficiency, MongoDB provides solid performance wherever you choose to deploy it.

Fitting Everything Together

Before we look at MongoDB's feature list, we need to review a few basic terms. MongoDB doesn't require much in the way of specialized knowledge to get started, and many of the terms specific to MongoDB can be loosely translated to RDBMS equivalents that you are probably already familiar with. Don't worry, though; we'll explain each term fully. Even if you're not familiar with standard database terminology, you will still be able to follow along easily.

Generating or Creating a Key

A document represents the unit of storage in MongoDB. In an RDBMS, this would be called a row. However, documents are much more than rows because they can store complex information such as lists, dictionaries, and even lists of dictionaries. In contrast to a traditional database where a row is fixed, a document in MongoDB can be made up of any number of keys and values (you'll learn more about this in the next section). Ultimately, a *key* is nothing more than a label; it is roughly equivalent to the name you might give to a column in an RDBMS. You use a key to reference pieces of data inside your document.

In a relational database, there should always be some way to uniquely identify a given record; otherwise it becomes impossible to refer to a specific row. To that end, you are supposed to include a field that holds a unique value (called a *primary key*) or a collection of fields that can uniquely identify the given row (called a *compound primary key*).

MongoDB requires that each document have a unique identifier for much the same reason; in MongoDB, this identifier is called _id. Unless you specify a value for this field, MongoDB will generate a unique value for you. Even in the well-established world of RDBMS databases, opinion is divided as to whether you should use a unique key provided by the database or generate a unique key yourself. Recently, it has become more popular to allow the database to create the key for you.

The reason for this is that human-created unique numbers such as car registration numbers have a nasty habit of changing. For example, in 2001, the United Kingdom implemented a new number plate scheme that was completely different from the previous system. It happens that MongoDB can cope with this type of change perfectly well; however, chances are that you would need to do some careful thinking if you used the registration plate as your primary key. A similar scenario may have occurred when the ISBN (International Standard Book Number) scheme was upgraded from 10 digits to 13.

Previously, most developers who used MongoDB seemed to prefer creating their own unique keys, taking it upon themselves to ensure that the number would remain unique. Today, though, general consensus seems to point at using the default ID value that MongoDB creates for you. However, as is the case when working with RDBMS databases, the approach you choose mostly comes down to personal preference. We prefer to use a database-provided value because it means we can be sure the key is unique and independent of anything else. Others, as noted, prefer to provide their own keys.

Ultimately, you must decide what works best for you. If you are confident that your key is unique (and likely to remain unchanged), then you should probably feel free to use it. If you're unsure about your key's uniqueness or you don't want to worry about it, then you can simply use the default key provided by MongoDB.

Using Keys and Values

Documents are made up of keys and values. Let's take another look at the example discussed previously in this chapter:

```
{
    "firstname": "Peter",
    "lastname": "Membrey",
    "phone_numbers": [
        "+852 1234 5678",
        "+44 1234 565 555"
    ]
}
```

Keys and values always come in pairs. Unlike an RDBMS, where every field must have a value, even if it's NULL (somewhat paradoxically, this means *unknown*), MongoDB doesn't require that a document have a particular value. For example, if you don't know the phone number for a particular person on your list, you simply leave it out. A popular analogy for this sort of thing is a business card. If you have a fax number, you usually put it on your business card; however, if you don't have one, you don't write: "Fax number: none." Instead, you simply leave the information out. If the key/value pair isn't included in a MongoDB document, it is assumed not to exist.

Implementing Collections

Collections are somewhat analogous to tables, but they are far less rigid. A collection is a lot like a box with a label on it. You might have a box at home labeled "DVDs" into which you put, well, your DVDs. This makes sense, but there is nothing stopping you from putting CDs or even tapes into this box if you wanted to. In an RDBMS, tables are strictly defined, and you can only put designated items into the table. In MongoDB, a collection is simply that: a collection of similar items. The items don't have to be similar (MongoDB is inherently flexible); however, once we start looking at indexing and more advanced queries, you'll soon see the benefits of placing similar items in a collection.

While you could mix various items together in a collection, there's little need to do so. Had the collection been called media, then all of the DVDs, CDs, and tapes would be at home there. After all, these items all have things in common, such as an artist name, a release date, and content. In other words, it really does depend on your application whether certain documents should be stored in the same collection. Performance-wise, having multiple collections is no slower than having only one collection. Remember: MongoDB is about making your life easier, so you should do whatever feels right to you.

Last but not least, collections are effectively created on demand. Specifically, a collection is created when you first attempt to save a document that references it. This means that you could create collections on demand (not that you necessarily should). Because MongoDB also lets you create indexes and perform other database-level commands dynamically, you can leverage this behavior to build some very dynamic applications.

Understanding Databases

Perhaps the easiest way to think of a database in MongoDB is as a collection of collections. Like collections, databases can be created on demand. This means that it's easy to create a database for each customer—your application code can even do it for you. You can do this with databases other than MongoDB, as well; however, creating databases in this manner with MongoDB is a very natural process. That said, just because you can create a database in this manner doesn't mean you have to or even that you should. All the same, you have that power if you want to exercise it.

Reviewing the Feature List

Now that you understand what MongoDB is and what it offers, it's time to run through its feature list. You can find a complete list of MongoDB's features on the database's website at www.mongodb.org/; be sure to visit this site for an up-to-date list of them. The feature list in this chapter covers a fair bit of material that goes on behind the scenes, but you don't need to be familiar with every feature listed to use MongoDB itself. In other words, if you feel your eyes beginning to close as you review this list, feel free to jump to the end of the section!

Using Document-Oriented Storage (BSON)

We've already discussed MongoDB's document-oriented design. We've also briefly touched on BSON. As you learned, JSON makes it much easier to store and retrieve documents in their real form, effectively removing the need for any sort of mapper or special conversion code. The fact that this feature also makes it much easier for MongoDB to scale up is icing on the cake.

BSON is an open standard; you can find its specification at http://bsonspec.org/. When people hear that BSON is a binary form of JSON, they expect it to take up much less room than text-based JSON. However, that isn't necessarily the case; indeed, there are many cases where the BSON version takes up more space than its JSON equivalent.

You might wonder why you should use BSON at all. After all, CouchDB (another powerful document-oriented database) uses pure JSON, and it's reasonable to wonder whether it's worth the trouble of converting documents back and forth between BSON and JSON.

First, we must remember that MongoDB is designed to be fast, rather than space-efficient. This doesn't mean that MongoDB wastes space (it doesn't); however, a small bit of overhead in storing a document is perfectly acceptable if that makes it faster to process the data (which it does). In short, BSON is much easier to *traverse* (that is, to look through) and index very quickly. Although BSON requires slightly more disk space than JSON, this extra space is unlikely to be a problem, because disks are cheap, and MongoDB can scale across machines. The tradeoff in this case is quite reasonable: you exchange a bit of extra disk space for better query and indexing performance.

The second key benefit to using BSON is that it is easy and quick to convert BSON to a programming language's native data format. If the data were stored in pure JSON, a relatively high-level conversion would need to take place. There are MongoDB drivers for a large number of programming languages (such as Python, Ruby, PHP, C, C++, and C#), and each works slightly differently. Using a simple binary format, native data structures can be quickly built for each language, without requiring that you first process JSON. This makes the code simpler and faster, both of which are in keeping with MongoDB's stated goals.

BSON also provides some extensions to JSON. For example, it enables you to store binary data and to incorporate a specific datatype. Thus, while BSON can store any JSON document, a valid BSON document may not be valid JSON. This doesn't matter, because each language has its own driver that converts data to and from BSON without needing to use JSON as an intermediary language.

At the end of the day, BSON is not likely to be a big factor in how you use MongoDB. Like all great tools, MongoDB will quietly sit in the background and do what it needs to do. Apart from possibly using a graphical tool to look at your data, you will generally work in your native language and let the driver worry about persisting to MongoDB.

Supporting Dynamic Queries

MongoDB's support for dynamic queries means that you can run a query without planning for it in advance. This is similar to being able to run SQL queries against an RDBMS. You might wonder why this is listed as a feature; surely it is something that every database supports—right?

Actually, no. For example, CouchDB (which is generally considered MongoDB's biggest "competitor") doesn't support dynamic queries. This is because CouchDB has come up with a completely new (and admittedly exciting) way of thinking about data. A traditional RDBMS has static data and dynamic queries. This means that the structure of the data is fixed in advance—tables must be defined, and each row has to fit into that structure. Because the database knows in advance how the data is structured, it can make certain assumptions and optimizations that enable fast dynamic queries.

CouchDB has turned this on its head. As a document-oriented database, CouchDB is schemaless, so the data is dynamic. However, the new idea here is that queries are static. That is, you define them in advance, before you can use them.

This isn't as bad as it might sound, because many queries can be easily defined in advance. For example, a system that lets you search for a book will probably let you search by ISBN. In CouchDB, you would create an index that builds a list of all the ISBNs for all the documents. When you punch in an ISBN, the query is very fast because it doesn't actually need to search for any data. Whenever new data is added to the system, CouchDB will automatically update its index.

Technically, you can run a query against CouchDB without generating an index; in that case, however, CouchDB will have to create the index itself before it can process your query. This won't be a problem if you only have a hundred books; however, it will result in poor performance if you're filing hundreds of thousands of books, because each query will generate the index again (and again). For this reason, the CouchDB team does not recommend dynamic queries—that is, queries that haven't been predefined—in production.

CouchDB also lets you write your queries as map and reduce functions. If that sounds like a lot of effort, then you're in good company; CouchDB has a somewhat severe learning curve. In fairness to CouchDB, an experienced programmer can probably pick it up quite quickly; for most people, however, the learning curve is probably steep enough that they won't bother with the tool.

Fortunately for us mere mortals, MongoDB is much easier to use. We'll cover how to use MongoDB in more detail throughout the book, but here's the short version: in MongoDB, you simply provide the parts of the document you want to match against, and MongoDB does the rest. MongoDB can do much more, however. For example, you won't find MongoDB lacking if you want to use map or reduce functions. At the same time, you can ease into using MongoDB; you don't have to know all of the tool's advanced features up front.

Indexing Your Documents

MongoDB includes extensive support for indexing your documents, a feature that really comes in handy when you're dealing with tens of thousands of documents. Without an index, MongoDB will have to look at each individual document in turn to see whether it is something that you want to see. This is like asking a librarian for a particular book and watching as he works his way around the library looking at each and every book. With an indexing system (libraries tend to use the Dewey Decimal system), he can find the area where the book you are looking for lives and very quickly determine if it is there.

Unlike a library book, all documents in MongoDB are automatically indexed on the _id key. This key is considered a special case because you cannot delete it; the index is what ensures that each value is unique. One of the benefits of this key is that you can be assured that each document is uniquely identifiable, something that isn't guaranteed by an RDBMS.

When you create your own indexes, you can decide whether you want them to enforce uniqueness. If you do decide to create a unique index, you can tell MongoDB to drop all the duplicates. This may or may not be what you want, so you should think carefully before using this option because you might accidentally delete half your data. By default, an error will be returned if you try to create a unique index on a key that has duplicate values.

There are many occasions where you will want to create an index that allows duplicates. For example, if your application searches by lastname, it makes sense to build an index on the lastname key. Of course, you cannot guarantee that each lastname will be unique; and in any database of a reasonable size, duplicates are practically guaranteed.

MongoDB's indexing abilities don't end there, however. MongoDB can also create indexes on embedded documents. For example, if you store numerous addresses in the address key, you can create an index on the ZIP or postal code. This means that you can easily pull back a document based on any postal code—and do so very quickly.

MongoDB takes this a step further by allowing *composite indexes*. In a composite index, two or more keys are used to build a given index. For example, you might build an index that combines both the lastname and firstname tags. A search for a full name would be very quick because MongoDB can quickly isolate the lastname and then, just as quickly, isolate the firstname.

We will look at indexing in more depth in Chapter 10, but suffice it to say that MongoDB has you covered as far as indexing is concerned.

Leveraging Geospatial Indexes

One form of indexing worthy of special mention is *geospatial indexing*. This new, specialized indexing technique was introduced in MongoDB 1.4. You use this feature to index location-based data, enabling you to answer queries such as how many items are within a certain distance from a given set of coordinates.

As an increasing number of web applications start making use of location-based data, this feature will play an increasingly prominent role in everyday development. For now, though, geospatial indexing remains a somewhat niche feature; nevertheless, you will be very glad it's there if you ever find that you need it.

Profiling Queries

A built-in profiling tool lets you see how MongoDB works out which documents to return. This is useful because, in many cases, a query can be easily improved simply by adding an index. If you have a complicated query, and you're not really sure why it's running so slowly, then the query profiler can provide you with extremely valuable information. Again, you'll learn more about the MongoDB Profiler in Chapter 10.

Updating Information In-Place

When a database updates a row (or in the case of MongoDB, a document), it has a couple of choices about how to do it. Many databases choose the multi-version concurrency control (MVCC) approach, which allows multiple users to see different versions of the data. This approach is useful because it ensures that the data won't be changed partway through by another program during a given transaction.

The downside to this approach is that the database needs to track multiple copies of the data. For example, CouchDB provides very strong versioning, but this comes at the cost of writing the data out in its entirety. While this ensures that the data is stored in a robust fashion, it also increases complexity and reduces performance.

MongoDB, on the other hand, updates information *in-place*. This means that (in contrast to CouchDB) MongoDB can update the data wherever it happens to be. This typically means that no extra space needs to be allocated, and the indexes can be left untouched.

Another benefit of this method is that MongoDB performs *lazy writes*. Writing to and from memory is very fast, but writing to disk is thousands of times slower. This means that you want to limit reading and writing from the disk as much as possible. This isn't possible in CouchDB, because that program ensures that each document is quickly written to disk. While this approach guarantees that the data is written safely to disk, it also impacts performance significantly.

MongoDB only writes to disk when it has to, which is usually once every second or so. This means that if a value is being updated many times a second—a not uncommon scenario if you're using a value as a page counter or for live statistics—then the value will only be written once, rather than the thousands of times that CouchDB would require.

This approach makes MongoDB much faster, but, again, it comes with a tradeoff. CouchDB may be slower, but it does guarantee that data is stored safely on the disk. MongoDB makes no such guarantee, and this is why a traditional RDBMS is probably a better solution for managing critical data such as billing or accounts receivable.

Storing Binary Data

GridFS is MongoDB's solution to storing binary data in the database. BSON supports saving up to 4MB of binary data in a document, and this may well be enough for your needs. For example, if you want to store a profile picture or a sound clip, then 4MB might be more space than you need. On the other hand, if you want to store movie clips, high-quality audio clips, or even files that are several hundred megabytes in size, then MongoDB has you covered here, too.

GridFS works by storing the information about the file (called *metadata*) in the files collection. The data itself is broken down into pieces called *chunks* that are stored in the chunks collection. This approach makes storing data both easy and scalable; it also makes range operations (such as retrieving specific parts of a file) much easier to use.

Generally speaking, you would use GridFS through your programming language's MongoDB driver, so it's unlikely you'd ever have to get your hands dirty at such a low level. As with everything else in MongoDB, GridFS is designed for both speed and scalability. This means you can be confident that MongoDB will be up to the task if you want to work with large data files.

Replicating Data

When we talked about the guiding principles behind MongoDB, we mentioned that RDBMS databases offer certain guarantees for data storage that are not available in MongoDB. These guarantees weren't implemented for a handful of reasons. First, these features would slow the database down. Second, they would greatly increase the complexity of the program. Third, it was felt that the most common failure on a server would be hardware, which would render the data unusable anyway, even if the data were safely saved to disk.

Of course, none of this means that data safety isn't important. MongoDB wouldn't be of much use if you couldn't count on being able to access the data when you need it. Initially, MongoDB provided a safety net with a feature called master-slave replication, in which only one database is active for writing at any given time, an approach that is also fairly common in the RDBMS world. This feature has since been replaced with *replica sets*, and basic master-slave replication has been deprecated and should no longer be used.

Replica sets have one primary server (similar to a master), which handles all the write requests from clients. Because there is only one primary server in a given set, it can guarantee that all writes are handled properly. When a write occurs it is logged in the primary's 'oplog'.

The oplog is replicated by the secondary servers (of which there can be many) and used to bring themselves up to date with the master. Should the master fail at any given time, one of the secondaries will become the primary and take over responsibility for handling client write requests.

Implementing Sharding

For those involved with large-scale deployments, auto-sharding will probably prove one of MongoDB's most significant and oft-used features.

In an *auto-sharding* scenario, MongoDB takes care of all the data splitting and recombination for you. It makes sure the data goes to the right server and that queries are run and combined in the most efficient manner possible. In fact, from a developer's point of view, there is no difference between talking to a MongoDB database with a hundred shards and talking to a single MongoDB server. This feature is not yet production-ready; when it is, however, it will push MongoDB's scalability through the roof.

In the meantime, if you're just starting out or you're building your first MongoDB-based website, then you'll probably find that a single instance of MongoDB is sufficient for your needs. If you end up building the next Facebook or Amazon, however, you will be glad that you built your site on a technology that can scale so limitlessly. Sharding is the topic of Chapter 12 of this book.

Using Map and Reduce Functions

For many people, hearing the term *MapReduce* sends shivers down their spines. At the other extreme, many RDBMS advocates scoff at the complexity of map and reduce functions. It's scary for some because these functions require a completely different way of thinking about finding and sorting your data, and many professional programmers have trouble getting their heads around the concepts that underpin map and reduce functions. That said, these functions provide an extremely powerful way to query data. In fact, CouchDB supports only this approach, which is one reason it has such a high learning curve.

MongoDB doesn't require that you use map and reduce functions. In fact, MongoDB relies on a simple querying syntax that is more akin to what you see in MySQL. However, MongoDB does make these functions available for those who want them. The map and reduce functions are written in JavaScript and run on the server. The job of the map function is to find all the documents that meet a certain criteria. These results are then passed to the reduce function, which processes the data. The reduce function doesn't usually return a collection of documents; rather, it returns a new document that contains the information derived. As a general rule, if you would normally use GROUP BY in SQL, then the map and reduce functions are probably the right tools for the job in MongoDB.

■ **Note** You should not think of MongoDB's map and reduce functions as poor imitations of the approach adopted by CouchDB. If you so desired, you could use MongoDB's map and reduce functions for everything in lieu of MongoDB's innate query support.

The MongoDB Aggregation Framework

MapReduce is a very powerful tool, but it has one major drawback; it's not exactly easy to use. Many database systems are used for reporting, and SQL databases in particular make this very easy. If you want to group results or find the maximum and average, then it's very simple to express that idea and get the result you're looking for. Unfortunately, it's not quite so simple to do that in MapReduce, and you effectively have to do all the wiring up yourself. This can often mean that an otherwise simple task is unnecessary challenging.

In response to this, MongoDB Inc (previously 10gen) added the aggregation framework. It is pipeline-based, similar to piping commands in Linux shells and allows you to take individual pieces of a query and string them together in order to get the result you're looking for. This maintains the benefits of MongoDB's document oriented design while still providing high performance.

So if you need all the power of MapReduce, you still have it at your beck and call. If you just want to do some basic statistics and number crunching, you're going to love the new aggregation framework. You'll learn more about the aggregation framework and its commands in Chapters 4 and 6.

Getting Help

MongoDB has a great community, and the core developers are very active and easily approachable, and they typically go to great lengths to help other members of the community. MongoDB is easy to use and comes with great documentation; however, it's still nice to know that you're not alone, and help is available, should you need it.

Visiting the Website

The first place to look for updated information or help is on the MongoDB website (`www://mongodb.org`). This site is updated regularly and contains all the latest MongoDB goodness. On this site, you can find drivers, tutorials, examples, frequently asked questions, and much more.

Chatting with the MongoDB Developers

The MongoDB developers hang out on Internet Relay Chat (IRC) at #MongoDB on the Freenode network (`www.freenode.net`). MongoDB's developers are based in New York, but they are often found chatting in this channel well into the night. Of course, the developers do need to sleep at some point (coffee only works for so long!); fortunately, there are also many knowledgeable MongoDB users from around the world who are ready to help out. Many people who visit the #MongoDB channel aren't experts; however, the general atmosphere is so friendly that they stick around anyway. Please feel free to join #MongoDB channel and chat with people there—you may find some great hints and tips. If you're really stuck, you'll probably be able to quickly get back on track.

Cutting and Pasting MongoDB Code

Pastie (`http://pastie.org`) is not strictly a MongoDB site; however, it is something you will come across if you float about in #MongoDB for any length of time. The Pastie site basically lets you cut and paste (hence the name) some output or program code, and then put it online for others to view. In IRC, pasting multiple lines of text can be messy or hard to read. If you need to post a fair bit of text (such as three lines or more), then you should visit `http://pastie.org`, paste in your content, and then paste the link to your new page into the channel.

Finding Solutions on Google Groups

MongoDB also has a Google group called `mongodb-user` (`http://groups.google.com/group/mongodb-user`). This group is a great place to ask questions or search for answers. You can also interact with the group via e-mail. Unlike IRC, which is very transient, the Google group is a great long-term resource. If you really want to get involved with the MongoDB community, joining the group is a great way to start.

Leveraging the JIRA Tracking System

MongoDB uses the JIRA issue-tracking system. You can view the tracking site at `http://jira.mongodb.org/`, and you are actively encouraged to report any bugs or problems that you come across to this site. Reporting such issues is viewed by the community as a genuinely good thing to do. Of course, you can also search through previous issues, and you can even view the roadmap and planned updates for the next release.

If you haven't posted to JIRA before, you might want to visit the IRC room first. You will quickly find out whether you've found something new, and if so, you will be shown how to go about reporting it.

Summary

This chapter has provided a whistle-stop tour of the benefits MongoDB brings to the table. We've looked at the philosophies and guiding principles behind MongoDB's creation and development, as well as the tradeoffs MongoDB's developers made when implementing these ideals. We've also looked at some of the key terms used in conjunction with MongoDB, how they fit together, and their rough SQL equivalents.

Next, we looked at some of the features MongoDB offers, including how and where you might want to use them. Finally, we wrapped up the chapter with a quick overview of the community and where you can go to get help, should you need it.

CHAPTER 2

■ ■ ■

Installing MongoDB

In Chapter 1, you got a taste of what MongoDB can do for you. In this chapter, you will learn how to install and expand MongoDB to do even more, enabling you to use it in combination with your favorite programming language.

MongoDB is a cross-platform database, and you can find a significant list of available packages to download from the MongoDB website (www.mongodb.org). The wealth of available versions might make it difficult to decide which version is the right one for you. The right choice for you probably depends on the operating system your server uses, the kind of processor in your server, and whether you prefer a stable release or would like to take a dive into a version that is still in development but offers exciting new features. Perhaps you'd like to install both a stable and a forward-looking version of the database. It's also possible you're not entirely sure which version you should choose yet. In any case, read on!

Choosing Your Version

When you look at the Download section on the MongoDB website, you will see a rather straightforward overview of the packages available for download. The first thing you need to pay attention to is the operating system you are going to run the MongoDB software on. Currently, there are precompiled packages available for Windows, various flavors of the Linux operating system, Mac OS, and Solaris.

■ **Note**   An important thing to remember here is the difference between the 32-bit release and the 64-bit release of the product. The 32-bit and 64-bit versions of the database currently have the same functionality, with one exception: the 32-bit release is limited to a total dataset size of approximately 2GB per server. The 64-bit version does not carry this restriction, however, so it's generally preferred over the 32-bit version for production environments. Also, the differences between these versions are subject to change.

You will also need to pay attention to the *version* of the MongoDB software itself: there are production releases, previous releases, and development releases. The *production* release indicates that it's the most recent stable version available. When a newer and generally improved or enhanced version is released, the prior most recent stable version will be made available as a *previous release*. This designation means the release is stable and reliable, but it usually has fewer features available in it. Finally, there's the *development release*. This release is generally referred to as the unstable version. This version is still in development, and it will include many changes, including significant new features. Although it has not been fully developed and tested yet, the developers of MongoDB have made it available to the public to test or otherwise try out.

Understanding the Version Numbers

MongoDB uses the "odd-numbered versions for development releases" approach. In other words, you can tell by looking at the second part of the version number (also called the release number) whether a version is a development version or a stable version. If the second number is even, then it's a *stable* release. If the second number is odd, then it's an *unstable*, or *development*, release.

Let's take a closer look at the three digits included in a version number's three parts, A, B, and C:

- A, the first (or leftmost) number: Represents the major version and only changes when there is a full version upgrade.

- B, the second (or middle) number: Represents the release number and indicates whether a version is a development version or a stable version. If the number is even, the version is stable; if the number is odd, the version is unstable and considered a development release.

- C, the third (or rightmost) number: Represents the revision number; this is used for bugs and security issues.

For example, at the time of writing, the following versions were available from the MongoDB website:

- 2.6.5 (Production release)

- 2.4.12 (Previous release)

- 2.7.8 (Development release)

Installing MongoDB on Your System

So far, you've learned which versions of MongoDB are available and—hopefully—were able to select one. Now you're ready to take a closer look at how to install MongoDB on your particular system. The two main operating systems for servers at the moment are based on Linux and Microsoft Windows, so this chapter will walk you through how to install MongoDB on both of these operating systems, beginning with Linux.

Installing MongoDB under Linux

The Unix-based operating systems are extremely popular choices at the moment for hosting services, including web services, mail services, and, of course, database services. In this chapter, we'll walk you through how to get MongoDB running on a popular Linux distribution: Ubuntu.

Depending on your needs, you have two ways of installing MongoDB under Ubuntu: you can install the packages automatically through so-called *repositories,* or you can install it manually. The next two sections will walk you through both options.

Installing MongoDB through the Repositories

Repositories are basically online directories filled with software. Every package contains information about the version number, prerequisites, and possible incompatibilities. This information is useful when you need to install a software package that requires another piece of software to be installed first because the prerequisites can be installed at the same time.

The default repositories available in Ubuntu (and other Debian-based distributions) contain MongoDB, but they may be out-of-date versions of the software. Therefore, let's tell apt-get (the software you use to install software from repositories) to look at a custom repository. To do this, you need to add the following line to your repository-list (/etc/apt/sources.list):

```
deb http://downloads-distro.mongodb.org/repo/ubuntu-upstart dist 10gen
```

Next, you need to import MongoDB Inc's public GPG key, used to sign the packages, ensuring their consistency; you can do so by using the apt-key command:

```
$ sudo apt-key adv --keyserver keyserver.ubuntu.com --recv 7F0CEB10
```

When that is done, you need to tell apt-get that it contains new repositories; you can do so using apt-get's update command:

```
$ sudo apt-get update
```

This line made aptitude aware of your manually added repository. This means you can now tell apt-get to install the software itself. You do this by typing the following command in the shell:

```
$ sudo apt-get install mongodb-org
```

This line installs the current stable (production) version from MongoDB. If you wish to install any other version from MongoDB instead, you need to specify the version number. For example, to install the current unstable (development) version from MongoDB, type in the following command instead:

```
$ sudo apt-get install mongodb-org=2.7.8
```

21

That's all there is to it. At this point, MongoDB has been installed and is (almost) ready to use!

■ **Note** Running `apt-get update` on a system running an older version of MongoDB will upgrade the software to the latest stable version available. You can prevent this from happening by running this command:

```
echo "mongodb-org hold" | sudo dpkg --set-selections
```

Installing MongoDB Manually

Next, we'll cover how to install MongoDB manually. Given how easy it is to install MongoDB with aptitude automatically, you might wonder why you would want to install the software manually. For starters, not all Linux distributions use apt-get. Sure, many of them do (including primarily the ones that are based on Debian Linux), but some don't. Also, the packaging remains a *work in progress*, so it might be the case that there are versions not yet available through the repositories. It's also possible that the version of MongoDB you want to use isn't included in the repository. Installing the software manually also gives you the ability to run multiple versions of MongoDB at the same time.

You've decided which version of MongoDB you would like to use, and you've downloaded it from their website, `http://mongodb.org/downloads`, to your Home directory. Next, you need to extract the package with the following command:

```
$ tar xzf mongodb-linux-x86_64-latest.tgz
```

This command extracts the entire contents of the package to a new directory called `mongodb-linux-x86_64-xxxx-yy-zz`; this directory is located under your current directory. This directory will contain a number of subdirectories and files. The directory that contains the executable files is called the `bin` directory. We will cover which applications perform which tasks shortly.

However, you don't need to do anything further to install the application. Indeed, it doesn't take much more time to install MongoDB manually—depending on what else you need to install, it might even be faster. Manually installing MongoDB does have some downsides, however. For example, the executables that you just extracted and found in the bin directory can't be executed from anywhere except the `bin` directory by default. Thus, if you want to run the `mongod` service, you will need to do so directly from the aforementioned `bin` directory. This downside highlights one of the benefits of installing MongoDB through repositories.

Installing MongoDB under Windows

Microsoft's Windows is also a popular choice for server software, including Internet-based services.

Windows doesn't come with a repository application like apt-get, so you'll need to download and extract the software from the MongoDB website to run it. Yes, the preceding information is correct. You do not need to walk through any setup process; installing the software is a simple matter of downloading the package, extracting it, and running the application itself.

For example, assume you've decided to download the latest stable version of MongoDB for your 64-bits Windows 2008 server. You begin by extracting the package (mongodb-win32-x86_64-x.y.x.zip) to the root of your C:\ drive. At this point, all you need to do is open a command prompt (Start ➤ Run ➤ cmd ➤ OK) and browse to the directory you extracted the contents to:

```
> cd C:\mongodb-win32-x86_64-x.y.z\
> cd bin\
```

Doing this brings you to the directory that contains the MongoDB executables. That's all there is to it: as I noted previously, no installation is necessary.

Running MongoDB

At long last, you're ready to get your hands dirty. You've learned where to get the MongoDB version that best suits your needs and hardware, and you've also seen how to install the software. Now it's finally time to look at running and using MongoDB.

Prerequisites

Before you can start the MongoDB service, you need to create a data directory for MongoDB to store its files in. By default, MongoDB stores the data in the /data/db directory on Unix-based systems (such as Linux and OS X) and in the C:\data\db directory on Windows.

■ **Note** MongoDB does not create these data directories for you, so you need to create them manually; otherwise, MongoDB will fail to run and throw an error message. Also, be sure that you set the permissions correctly: MongoDB must have read, write, and directory creation permissions to function properly.

If you wish to use a directory other than /data/db or C:\data\db, then you can tell MongoDB to look at the desired directory by using the --dbpath flag when executing the service.

Once you create the required directory and assign the appropriate permissions, you can start the MongoDB core database service by executing the *mongod* application. You can do this from the command prompt or the shell in Windows and Linux, respectively.

Surveying the Installation Layout

After you install or extract MongoDB successfully, you will have the applications shown in Table 2-1 available in the bin directory (in both Linux and Windows).

Table 2-1. *The Included MongoDB Applications*

Application	Function
-- bsondump	Reads contents of BSON-formatted rollback files.
-- mongo	The database shell.
-- mongod	The core database server.
-- mongodump	Database backup utility.
-- mongoexport	Export utility (JSON, CSV, TSV), not reliable for backup.
-- mongofiles	Manipulates files in GridFS objects.
-- mongoimport	Import utility (JSON, CSV, TSV), not reliable for recoveries.
-- mongooplog	Pulls oplog entries from another mongod instance.
-- mongoperf	Check disk I/O performance.
--mongorestore	Database backup restore utility.
--mongos	Mongodb sharding routerprocess.
--mongosniff	Sniff/traces MongoDB database activity in real time, Unix-like systems only.
--mongostat	Returns counters of database operation.
--mongotop	Tracks/reports MongoDB read/write activities.
-- mongorestore	Restore/import utility.

Note: All applications are within the --bin directory.

The installed software includes 15 applications (or 14, under Microsoft Windows) that you will be using in conjunction with your MongoDB databases. The two "most important" applications are the mongo and mongod applications. The mongo application allows you to use the database shell; this shell enables you to accomplish practically anything you'd want to do with MongoDB.

The mongod application starts the service or *daemon*, as it's also called. There are also many flags you can set when launching the MongoDB applications. For example, the service lets you specify the path where the database is located (--dbpath), show version information (--version), and even print some diagnostic system information (with the --sysinfo flag)! You can view the entire list of options by including the --help flag when you launch the service. For now, you can just use the defaults and start the service by typing mongod in your shell or command prompt.

Using the MongoDB Shell

Once you create the database directory and start the mongod database application successfully, you're ready to fire up the shell and take a sneak peak at the powers of MongoDB.

Fire up your shell (Unix) or your command prompt (Windows); when you do so, make sure you are in the correct location, so that the mongo executable can be found. You can start the shell by typing mongo at the command prompt and hitting the Return key. You will be immediately presented with a blank window and a blinking cursor (see Figure 2-1). Ladies and gentlemen, welcome to MongoDB!

```
MongoDB
MongoDB shell version: 2.5.1-pre-
connecting to: test
>
```

Figure 2-1. *The MongoDB shell*

If you start the MongoDB service with the default parameters, and start the shell with the default settings, you will be connected to the default test database running on your local host. This database is created automatically the moment you connect to it. This is one of MongoDB's most powerful features: if you attempt to connect to a database that does not exist, MongoDB will automatically create it for you. This can be either good or bad, depending on how well you handle your keyboard.

■ **Tip**   There's an on-line demo shell available on the MongoDB website where you can try out any of the commands listed.

Before taking any further steps, such as implementing any additional drivers that will enable you to work with your favorite programming language, you might find it helpful to take a quick peek at some of the more useful commands available in the MongoDB shell (see Table 2-2).

Table 2-2. Basic Commands within the MongoDB Shell

Command	Function
show dbs	Shows the names of the available databases.
show collections	Shows the collections in the current database.
show users	Shows the users in the current database.
use <db name>	Sets the current database to <db name>.

■ **Tip** You can get a full list of commands by typing the help command in the MongoDB shell.

Installing Additional Drivers

You might think that you are ready to take on the world now that you have set up MongoDB and know how to use its shell. That's partially true; however, you probably want to use your preferred programming language rather than the shell when querying or otherwise manipulating the MongoDB database. 10gen offers multiple official drivers, and many more are offered in the community that let you do precisely that. For example, drivers for the following programming languages can be found on the MongoDB website:

- C
- C++
- C#
- Erlang
- Go
- Java
- JavaScript
- Node.js
- Perl
- PHP
- Python
- Ruby
- Scala

In this section, you will learn how to implement MongoDB support for two of the more popular programming languages in use today: PHP and Python.

■ **Tip** There are many community-driven MongoDB drivers available. A long list can be found on the MongoDB website, www.mongodb.org.

Installing the PHP Driver

PHP is one of the most popular programming languages in existence today. This language is specifically aimed at web development, and it can be incorporated into HTML easily. This fact makes the language the perfect candidate for designing a web application, such as a blog, a guestbook, or even a business-card database. The next few sections cover your options for installing and using the MongoDB PHP driver.

Getting MongoDB for PHP

Like MongoDB, PHP is a cross-platform development tool, and the steps required to set up MongoDB in PHP vary depending on the intended platform. Previously, this chapter showed you how to install MongoDB on both Ubuntu and Windows; we'll adopt the same approach here, demonstrating how to install the driver for PHP on both Ubuntu and Windows.

Begin by downloading the PHP driver for your operating system. Do this by firing up your browser and navigating to www.mongodb.org. At the time of writing, the website includes a separate menu option called Drivers. Click this option to bring up a list of currently available language drivers (see Figure 2-2).

MongoDB Ecosystem

MongoDB Drivers
  C Driver
  C++ Driver
  C# and .NET Driver
  Java Driver
  Node.js Driver
  Perl Driver
  PHP Driver
  Python Driver
  Ruby Driver
  Scala Driver
  Go Driver
  Erlang Driver
  Other Community Supported Drivers
  Driver Syntax Table

MongoDB Drivers

Drivers

Community Supported Drivers

 • Other Community Supported Drivers

Driver Syntax Table

 • Driver Syntax Table

Figure 2-2. *A short list of currently available language drivers for MongoDB*

Next, select PHP from the list of languages and follow the links to download the latest (stable) version of the driver. Different operating systems will require different approaches for installing the MongoDB extension for PHP automatically. That's right; just as you were able to install MongoDB on Ubuntu automatically, you can do the same for the PHP driver. And just as when installing MongoDB under Ubuntu, you can also choose to install the PHP language driver manually. Let's look at the two options available to you.

Installing the PHP Driver on Unix-Based Platforms Automatically

The developers of PHP came up with a great solution that allows you to expand your PHP installation with other popular extensions: *PECL*. PECL is a repository solely designed for PHP; it provides a directory of all known extensions that you can use to download, install, and even develop PHP extensions. If you are already acquainted with the package-management system called aptitude (which you used previously to install MongoDB), then you will be pleased by how similar PECL's interface is to the one in aptitude.

Assuming that you have PECL installed on your system, open up a console and type the following command to install the MongoDB extension:

```
$ sudo pecl install mongo
```

Entering this command causes PECL to download and install the MongoDB extension for PHP automatically. In other words, PECL will download the extension for your PHP version and place it in the PHP extensions directory. There's just one catch: PECL does not automatically add the extension to the list of loaded extensions; you will need to do this step manually. To do so, open a text editor (vim, nano, or whichever text editor you prefer) and alter the file called php.ini, which is the main configuration file PHP uses to control its behavior, including the extensions it should load.

Next, open the php.ini file, scroll down to the extensions section, and add the following line to tell PHP to load the MongoDB driver:

```
extension=mongo.so
```

■ **Note** The preceding step is mandatory; if you don't do this, then the MongoDB commands in PHP will not function. To find the php.ini file on your system, you can use the grep command in your shell: php -i | grep Configuration.

The "Confirming That Your PHP Installation Works" section later in this chapter will cover how to confirm that an extension has been loaded successfully.

That's all, folks! You've just installed the MongoDB extension for your PHP installation, and you are now ready to use it. Next, you will learn how to install the driver manually.

Installing the PHP Driver on Unix-Based Platforms Manually

If you would prefer to compile the driver yourself or for some reason are unable to use the PECL application as described previously (your hosting provider might not support this option, for instance), then you can also choose to download the source driver and compile it manually.

To download the driver, go to the github website (http://github.com). This site offers the latest source package for the PHP driver. Once you download it, you will need to extract the package, and *make* the driver by running the following set of commands:

```
$ tar zxvf mongodb-mongodb-php-driver-<commit_id>.tar.gz
$ cd mongodb-mongodb-php-driver-<commit_id>
$ phpize
$ ./configure
$ sudo make install
```

This process can take a while, depending on the speed of your system. Once the process completes, your MongoDB PHP driver is installed and ready to use! After you execute the commands, you will be shown where the driver has been placed; typically, the output looks something like this:

```
Installing '/ usr/lib/php/extensions/no-debug-zts-20060613/mongo.so'
```

You do need to confirm that this directory is the same directory where PHP stores its extensions by default. You can use the following command to confirm where PHP stores its extensions:

```
$ php -i | grep extension_dir
```

This line outputs the directory where all PHP extensions should be placed. If this directory doesn't match the one where the mongo.so driver was placed, then you must move the mongo.so driver to the proper directory, so PHP knows where to find it.

As before, you will need to tell PHP that the newly created extension has been placed in its extension directory, and that it should load this extension. You can specify this by modifying the php.ini file's extensions section; add the following line to that section:

```
extension=mongo.so
```

Finally, a restart of your web service is required. When using the Apache HTTPd service, you can accomplish this using the following service command:

```
sudo /etc/init.d/apache2 restart
```

That's it! This process is a little lengthier than using PECL's automated method; however, if you are unable to use PECL, or if you are a driver developer and interested in bug fixes, then you would want to use the manual method instead.

Installing the PHP Driver on Windows

You have seen previously how to install MongoDB on your Windows operating system. Now let's look at how to implement the MongoDB driver for PHP on Windows.

For Windows, there are precompiled binaries available for each release of the PHP driver for MongoDB. You can get these binaries from the previously mentioned github website (http://github.com). The biggest challenge in this case is choosing the correct package to install for your version of PHP (a wide variety of packages are available). If you aren't certain which package version you need, you can use the `<? phpinfo(); ?>` command in a PHP page to learn exactly which one suits your specific environment. We'll take a closer look at the phpinfo() command in the next section.

After downloading the correct package and extracting its contents, all you need to do is copy the driver file (called php_mongo.dll) to your PHP's extension directory; this enables PHP to pick it up.

Depending on your version of PHP, the extension directory may be called either Ext or Extensions. If you aren't certain which directory it should be, you can review the PHP documentation that came with the version of PHP installed on your system.

Once you place the driver DLL into the PHP extensions directory, you still need to tell PHP to load the driver. Do this by altering the php.ini file and adding the following line in the extensions section:

```
extension=php_mongo.dll
```

When done, restart the HTTP service on your system, and you are now ready to use the MongoDB driver in PHP. Before you start leveraging the magic of MongoDB with PHP, however, you need to confirm that the extension is loaded correctly.

Confirming That Your PHP Installation Works

So far you've successfully installed both MongoDB and the MongoDB driver in PHP. Now it's time to do a quick check to confirm whether the driver is being loaded correctly by PHP. PHP gives you a simple and straightforward method to accomplish this: the phpinfo() command. This command shows you an extended overview of all the modules loaded, including version numbers, compilation options, server information, OS information, and so on.

To use the phpinfo() command, open a text or HTML editor and type the following:

```
<? phpinfo(); ?>
```

Next, save the document in your webserver's www directory and call it whatever you like. For example, you might call it test.php or phpinfo.php. Now open your browser and go to your localhost or external server (that is, go to whatever server you are working on) and look at the page you just created. You will see a good overview of all PHP components and all sorts of other relevant information. The thing you need to focus on here is the section that displays your MongoDB information. This section will list the version number, port numbers, hostname, and so on (see Figure 2-3).

mongo

MongoDB Support		enabled
Version		1.3.2

Directive	Local Value	Master Value
mongo.allow_empty_keys	0	0
mongo.chunk_size	262144	262144
mongo.cmd	$	$
mongo.default_host	localhost	localhost
mongo.default_port	27017	27017
mongo.is_master_interval	*no value*	*no value*
mongo.long_as_object	0	0
mongo.native_long	0	0
mongo.ping_interval	*no value*	*no value*
mongo.utf8	1	1

Figure 2-3. *Displaying your MongoDB information in PHP*

Once you confirm that the installation was successful and that the driver loaded successfully, you're ready to write some PHP code and walk through a MongoDB example that leverages PHP.

Connecting to and Disconnecting from the PHP Driver

You've confirmed that the MongoDB PHP driver has been loaded correctly, so it's time to start writing some PHP code! Let's take a look at two simple yet fundamental options for working with MongoDB: initiating a connection between MongoDB and PHP, and then severing that connection.

You use the Mongo class to initiate a connection between MongoDB and PHP; this same class also lets you use the database server commands. A simple yet typical connection command looks like this:

```
$connection = new Mongo();
```

If you use this command without providing any parameters, it will connect to the MongoDB service on the default MongoDB port (27017) on your localhost. If your MongoDB service is running somewhere else, then you simply specify the hostname of the remote host you want to connect to:

```
$connection = new Mongo("example.com");
```

This line instantiates a fresh connection for your MongoDB service running on the server and listening to the example.com domain name (note that it will still connect to the default port: 27017). If you want to connect to a different port number, however (for example, if you don't want to use the default port, or you're already running another session of the MongoDB service on that port), you can do so by specifying the port number and hostname:

```
$connection = new Mongo("example.com:12345");
```

This example creates a connection to the database service. Next, you will learn how to disconnect from the service. Assuming you used the method just described to connect to your database, you can call $connection again to pass the close() command to terminate the connection, as in this example:

```
$connection->close();
```

The close doesn't need to be called, except in unusual circumstances. The reason for this is that the PHP driver closes the connection to the database once the Mongo object goes out of scope. Nevertheless, it is recommended that you call close() at the end of your PHP code; this helps you avoid keeping old connections from hanging around until they eventually time out. It also helps you ensure that any existing connection is closed, thereby enabling a new connection to happen, as in the following example:

```
$connection = new Mongo();
$connection->close();
$connection->connect();
```

The following snippet shows how this would look like in PHP:

```
<?php

// Establish the database connection
$connection = new Mongo()

// Close the database connection
$connection->close();

?>
```

Installing the Python Driver

Python is a general-purpose and easy-to-read programming language.

These qualities make Python a good language to start with when you are new to programming and scripting. It's also a great language to look into if you are familiar with programming, and you're looking for a multi-paradigm programming language that permits several styles of programming (object-oriented programming, structured programming, and so on). In the upcoming sections, you'll learn how to install Python and enable MongoDB support for the language.

Installing PyMongo under Linux

Python offers a specific package for MongoDB support called PyMongo. This package allows you to interact with the MongoDB database, but you will need to get this driver up and running before you can use this powerful combination. As when installing the PHP driver, there are two methods you can use to install PyMongo: an automated approach that relies on setuptools or a manual approach where you download the source code for the project. The following sections show you how to install PyMongo using both approaches.

Installing PyMongo Automatically

The `pip` application that comes bundled with the `python-pip` package lets you automatically download, build, install, and manage Python packages. This is incredibly convenient, enabling you to extend your Python modules installation even as it does all the work for you.

■ **Note**   You must have setuptools installed before you can use the `pip` application. This will be done automatically when installing the python-pip package.

To install `pip`, all you need to do is tell `apt-get` to download and install it, like so:

```
$ sudo apt-get install python-pip
```

When this line executes, `pip` will detect the currently running version of Python and installs itself on the system. That's all there is to it. Now you are ready to use the `pip` command to download, make, and install the MongoDB module, as in this example:

```
$ sudo pip install pymongo
```

Again, that's all there is to it! PyMongo is now installed and ready to use.

■ **Tip**   You can also install previous versions of the PyMongo module with pip using the `pip install pymongo=x.y.z` command. Here, x.y.z denotes the version of the module.

Installing PyMongo Manually

You can also choose to install PyMongo manually. Begin by going to the download section of the site that hosts the PyMongo plugin (`http://pypi.python.org/pypi/pymongo`). Next, download the tarball and extract it. A typical download and extract procedure might look like this in your console:

```
$ wget http://pypi.python.org/packages/source/p/pymongo/pymongo-2.5.1.tar.gz
$ tar xzf pymongo-2.5.1.tar.gz
```

Once you successfully download and extract this file, make your way to the extracted contents directory and invoke the installation of PyMongo by running the install.py command with Python:

```
$ cd pymongo-2.5.1
$ sudo python setup.py install
```

The preceding snippet outputs the entire creation and installation process of the PyMongo module. Eventually, this process brings you back to your prompt, at which time you're ready to start using PyMongo.

Installing PyMongo under Windows

Installing PyMongo under Windows is a straightforward process. As when installing PyMongo under Linux, Easy Install can simplify installing PyMongo under Windows as well. If you don't have setuptools installed yet (this package includes the easy_install command), then go to the Python Package Index website (http://pypi.python.org) to locate the setuptools installer.

■ **Caution**   The version of setuptools you download must match the version of Python installed on your system.

For example, assume you have Python version 2.7.5 installed on your system. You will need to download the setuptools package for v2.7.x. The good news is that you don't need to compile any of this; rather, you can simply download the appropriate package and double-click the executable to install setuptools on your system! It is that simple.

■ **Caution**   If you have previously installed an older version of setuptools, then you will need to uninstall that version using your system's Add/Remove Programs feature *before* installing the newer version.

Once the installation is complete, you will find the easy_install.exe file in Python's Scripts subdirectory. At this point, you're ready to install PyMongo on Windows.

Once you've successfully installed setuptools, you can open a command prompt and cd your way to Python's Scripts directory. By default, this is set to C:\Pythonxy\Scripts\, where xy represents your version number. Once you navigate to this location, you can use the same syntax shown previously for installing the Unix variant:

```
C:\Python27\Scripts> easy_install PyMongo
```

Unlike the output that you get when installing this program on a Linux machine, the output here is rather brief, indicating only that the extension has been downloaded and installed (see Figure 2-4). That said, this information is sufficient for your purposes in this case.

Figure 2-4. *Installing PyMongo under Windows*

Confirming That Your PyMongo Installation Works

To confirm whether the PyMongo installation has completed successfully, you can open up your Python shell. In Linux, you do this by opening a console and typing python. In Windows, you do this by clicking Start ➤ Programs ➤ Python *xy* ➤ Python (commandline). At this point, you will be welcomed to the world of Python (see Figure 2-5).

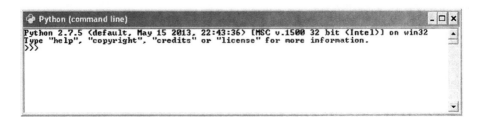

Figure 2-5. *The Python shell*

You can use the import command to tell Python to start using the freshly installed extension:

```
>>> import pymongo
>>>
```

▨ **Note** You must use the `import pymongo` command each time you want to use PyMongo.

If all went well, you will not see a thing, and you can start firing off some fancy MongoDB commands. If you received an error message, however, something went wrong, and you might need to review the steps just taken to discover where the error occurred.

Summary

In this chapter, we examined how to obtain the MongoDB software, including how to select the correct version you need for your environment. We also discussed the version numbers, how to install and run MongoDB, and how to install and run its prerequisites. Next, we covered how to establish a connection to a database through a combination of the shell, PHP, and Python.

We also explored how to expand MongoDB so it will work with your favorite programming languages, as well as how to confirm whether the language-specific drivers have installed correctly.

In the next chapter, we will explore how to design and structure MongoDB databases and data properly. Along the way, you'll learn how to index information to speed up queries, how to reference data, and how to leverage a fancy new feature called *geospatial indexing*.

CHAPTER 3

■ ■ ■

The Data Model

In the previous chapter, you learned how to install MongoDB on two commonly used platforms (Windows and Linux), as well as how to extend the database with some additional drivers. In this chapter, you will shift your attention from the operating system and instead examine the general design of a MongoDB database. Specifically, you'll learn what collections are, what documents look like, how indexes work and what they do, and finally, when and where to reference data instead of embedding it. We touched on some of these concepts briefly in Chapter 1, but in this chapter, we'll explore them in more detail. Throughout this chapter, you will see code examples designed to give you a good feeling for the concepts being discussed. Do not worry too much about the commands you'll be looking at, however, because they will be discussed extensively in Chapter 4.

Designing the Database

As you learned in the first two chapters, a MongoDB database is nonrelational and schemaless. This means that a MongoDB database isn't bound to any predefined columns or datatypes as relational databases are (such as MySQL). The biggest benefit of this implementation is that working with data is extremely flexible because there is no predefined structure required in your documents.

To put it more simply: you are perfectly capable of having one collection that contains hundreds or even thousands of documents that all carry a different structure—without breaking any of the MongoDB databases rules.

One of the benefits of this flexible schemaless design is that you won't be restricted when programming in a dynamically typed language such as Python or PHP. Indeed, it would be a severe limitation if your extremely flexible and dynamically capable programming language couldn't be used to its full potential because of the innate limitations of your database.

Let's take another glance at what the data design of a document in MongoDB looks like, paying particular attention to how flexible data in MongoDB is compared to data in a relational database. In MongoDB, a *document* is an item that contains the actual data, comparable to a row in SQL. In the following example, you will see how two completely different types of documents can coexist in a single collection named Media (note that a *collection* is roughly equivalent to a table in the world of SQL):

```
{
    "Type": "CD",
    "Artist": "Nirvana",
    "Title": "Nevermind",
    "Genre": "Grunge",
    "Releasedate": "1991.09.24",
    "Tracklist": [
        {
        "Track" : "1",
        "Title" : "Smells Like Teen Spirit",
        "Length" : "5:02"
        },
        {
        "Track" : "2",
        "Title" : "In Bloom",
        "Length" : "4:15"
        }
    ]
}

{
    "type": "Book",
    "Title": "Definitive Guide to MongoDB: A complete guide to dealing with
    Big Data using MongoDB 2nd , The",
    "ISBN": "987-1-4302-5821-6",
    "Publisher": "Apress",
    "Author": [
        "Hows, David"
        "Plugge, Eelco",
        "Membrey, Peter",
        "Hawkins, Tim     ]
}
```

As you might have noticed when looking at this pair of documents, most of the fields aren't closely related to one another. Yes, they both have fields called Title and Type; but apart from that similarity, the documents are completely different. Nevertheless, these two documents are contained in a single collection called Media.

MongoDB is called a *schemaless* database, but that doesn't mean MongoDB's data structure is completely devoid of schema. For example, you do define collections and indexes in MongoDB (you will learn more about this later in the chapter). Nevertheless, you do not *need* to predefine a structure for any of the documents you will be adding, as is the case when working with MySQL, for example.

Simply stated, MongoDB is an extraordinarily dynamic database; the preceding example would never work in a relational database, unless you also added each possible field to your table. Doing so would be a waste of both space and performance, not to mention highly disorganized.

Drilling Down on Collections

As mentioned previously, *collection* is a commonly used term in MongoDB. You can think of a collection as a container that stores your documents (that is, your data), as shown in Figure 3-1.

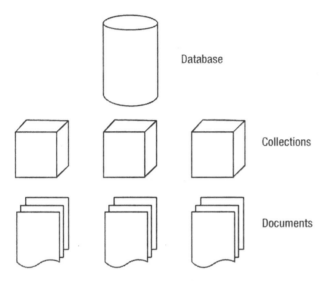

Figure 3-1. *The MongoDB database model*

Now compare the MongoDB database model to a typical model for a relational database (see Figure 3-2).

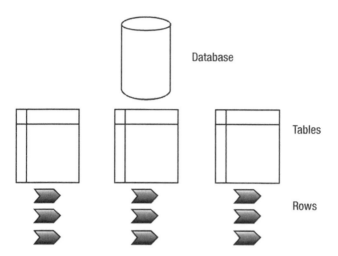

Figure 3-2. *A typical relational database model*

As you can see, the general structure is the same between the two types of databases; nevertheless, you do not use them in even remotely similar manners. There are several types of collections in MongoDB. The default collection type is expandable in size: the more data you add to it, the larger it becomes. It's also possible to define collections that are *capped*. These *capped collections* can only contain a certain amount of data before the oldest document is replaced by a newer document (you will learn more about these collections in Chapter 4).

Every collection in MongoDB has a unique name. This name should begin with a letter, or optionally, an underscore (_) when created using the createCollection function. The name can contain numbers and letters; however, the $ symbol is reserved by MongoDB. Similarly, using an empty string (" ") is not allowed; the null character cannot be used in the name and it cannot start with the "system." string. Generally, it's recommended that you keep the collection's name simple and short (to around nine characters or so); however, the maximum number of allowed characters in a collection name is 118, minus the number of charaters in the database and the additional separating period character. Obviously, there isn't much practical reason to create such a long name.

The above mentioned combination of databasename "period" collection name is called a namespace. A single database has a default limit of 24,000 namespaces. Each collection accounts for at least two namespaces: one for the collection itself and one more for the default _id index created in the collection. If you were to add more indexes per collection, however, another namespace would be used. In theory, this means that each database can have up to 12,000 collections by default, assuming each collection only carries one index. However, this limit on the number of namespaces can be increased by providing the nssize parameter when executing the MongoDB service application (mongod).

Using Documents

Recall that a *document* consists of key-value pairs. For example, the pair "type" : "Book" consists of a key named type, and its value, Book. Keys are written as *strings*, but the values in them can vary tremendously. Values can be any of a rich set of datatypes, such as arrays or even binary data. Remember: MongoDB stores its data in BSON format (see Chapter 1 for more information on this topic).

Next, let's look at all of the possible types of data you can add to a document, and what you use them for:

- *String*: This commonly used datatype contains a string of text (or any other kind of characters). This datatype is used mostly for storing text values (for example, "Country" : "Japan"}.

- *Integer (32b and 64b)*: This type is used to store a numerical value (for example, { "Rank" : 1 }). Note that there are no quotes placed before or after the integer.

- *Boolean*: This datatype can be set to either TRUE or FALSE.

- *Double*: This datatype is used to store floating-point values.

- *Min / Max keys*: This datatype is used to compare a value against the lowest and highest BSON elements, respectively.

- *Arrays*: This datatype is used to store arrays (for example, ["Membrey, Peter","Plugge, Eelco","Hows, David"]).

- *Timestamp*: This datatype is used to store a timestamp. This can be handy for recording when a document has been modified or added.

- *Object*: This datatype is used for embedded documents.

- *Null*: This datatype is used for a Null value.

- *Symbol*: This datatype is used identically to a string; however, it's generally reserved for languages that use a specific symbol type.

- *Date **: This datatype is used to store the current date or time in Unix time format (POSIX time).

- *Object ID **: This datatype is used to store the document's ID.

- *Binary data **: This datatype is used to store binary data.

- *Regular expression **: This datatype is used for regular expressions. All options are represented by specific characters provided in alphabetical order. You will learn more about regular expressions in Chapter 4.

- *JavaScript Code **: This datatype is used for JavaScript code.

The asterisks mean that the last five datatypes (date, object ID, binary data, regex, and JavaScript code) are non-JSON types; specifically, they are special datatypes that BSON allows you to use. In Chapter 4, you will learn how to identify your datatypes by using the $type operator.

In theory, this all probably sounds straightforward. However, you might wonder how you go about actually designing the document, including what information to put in it. Because a document can contain any type of data, you might think there is no need to reference information from inside another document. In the next section, we'll look at the pros and cons of embedding information in a document compared to referencing that information from another document.

Embedding vs. Referencing Information in Documents

You can choose either to embed information into a document or reference that information from another document. Embedding information simply means that you place a certain type of data (for example, an array containing more data) into the document itself. Referencing information means that you create a reference to another document that contains that specific data. Typically, you reference information when you use a relational database. For example, assume you wanted to use a relational database to keep track of your CDs, DVDs, and books. In this database, you might have one table for your CD collection and another table that stores the track lists of your CDs. Thus, you would probably need to query multiple tables to acquire a list of tracks from a specific CD.

With MongoDB (and other nonrelational databases), however, it would be much easier to embed such information instead. After all, the documents are natively capable of doing so. Adopting this approach keeps your database nice and tidy, ensures that all related information is kept in one single document, and even works much faster because the data is then co-located on the disk.

Now let's look at the differences between embedding and referencing information by looking at a real-world scenario: storing CD data in a database.

In the relational approach, your data structure might look something like this:

```
|_media
    |_cds
        |_id, artist, title, genre, releasedate
    |_ cd_tracklists
        |_cd_id, songtitle, length
```

In the nonrelational approach, your data structure might look something like this:

```
|_media
    |_items
        |_<document>
```

In the nonrelational approach, the document might look something like the following:

```
{
    "Type": "CD",
    "Artist": "Nirvana",
    "Title": "Nevermind",
    "Genre": "Grunge",
    "Releasedate": "1991.09.24",
    "Tracklist": [
        {
        "Track" : "1",
        "Title" : "Smells Like Teen Spirit",
        "Length" : "5:02"
        },
        {
        "Track" : "2",
        "Title" : "In Bloom",
        "Length" : "4:15"
        }
    ]
}
```

In this example, the track list information is embedded in the document itself. This approach is both incredibly efficient and well organized. All the information that you wish to store regarding this CD is added to a single document. In the relational version of the CD database, this requires at least two tables; in the nonrelational database, it requires only one collection and one document.

When information is retrieved for a given CD, that information only needs to be loaded from one document into RAM, not from multiple documents. Remember that every reference requires another query in the database.

■ **Tip** The rule of thumb when using MongoDB is to embed data whenever you can. This approach is far more efficient and almost always viable.

At this point, you might be wondering about the use case in which an application has multiple users. Generally speaking, a relational database version of the aforementioned CD app would require that you have one table that contains all your users and two tables for the items added. For a nonrelational database, it would be good practice to have separate collections for the users and the items added. For these kinds of problems, MongoDB allows you to create references in two ways: manually or automatically. In the latter case, you use the DBRef specification, which provides more flexibility in case a collection changes from one document to the next. You will learn more about these two approaches in Chapter 4.

Creating the _id Field

Every object within the MongoDB database contains a unique identifier to distinguish that object from every other object. This identifier is called the _id key, and it is added automatically to every document you create in a collection.

The _id key is the first attribute added in each new document you create. This remains true even if you do not tell MongoDB to create the key. For example, none of the code in the preceding examples used the _id key. Nevertheless, MongoDB created an _id key for you automatically in each document. It did so because _id key is a mandatory element for each document in the collection.

If you do not specify the _id value manually, the type will be set to a special BSON datatype that consists of a 12-byte binary value. Thanks to its design, this value has a reasonably high probability of being unique. The 12-byte value consists of a 4-byte timestamp (seconds since epoch, or January 1st, 1970), a 3-byte machine ID, a 2-byte process ID, and a 3-byte counter. It's good to know that the counter and timestamp fields are stored in *Big Endian* format. This is because MongoDB wants to ensure that there is an increasing order to these values, and a Big Endian approach suits this requirement best.

■ **Note**   The terms *Big Endian* and *Little Endian* refer to how individual bytes/bits are stored in a longer data word in the memory. Big Endian simply means that the most significant value is saved first. Similarly, Little Endian means that the least significant value is saved first.

Figure 3-3 shows how the value of the _id key is built up and where the values come from.

0	1	2	3	4	5	6	7	8	9	10	11
Time				machine			Pid		inc		

Figure 3-3. *Creating the _id key in MongoDB*

Every additional supported driver that you load when working with MongoDB (such as the PHP driver or the Python driver) supports this special BSON datatype and uses it whenever new data is created. You can also invoke ObjectId() from the MongoDB shell to create a value for an _id key. Optionally, you can specify your own value by using ObjectId(*string*), where *string* represents the specified hex string.

Building Indexes

As mentioned in Chapter 1, an *index* is nothing more than a data structure that collects information about the values of specified fields in the documents of a collection. This data structure is used by MongoDB's query optimizer to quickly sort through and order the documents in a collection.

Remember that indexing ensures a quick lookup from data in your documents. Basically, you should view an index as a predefined query that was executed and had its results stored. As you can imagine, this enhances query-performance dramatically. The general rule of thumb in MongoDB is that you should create an index for the same sort of scenarios where you would want to have an index in MySQL.

The biggest benefit of creating your own indexes is that querying for often-used information will be incredibly fast because your query won't need to go through your entire database to collect this information.

Creating (or deleting) an index is relatively easy—once you get the hang of it, anyway. You will learn how to do so in Chapter 4, which covers working with data. You will also learn some more advanced techniques for taking advantage of indexing in Chapter 10, which covers how to maximize performance.

Impacting Performance with Indexes

You might wonder why you would ever need to delete an index, rebuild your indexes, or even delete all indexes within a collection. The simple answer is that doing so lets you clean up some irregularities. For instance, sometimes the size of a database can increase dramatically for no apparent reason. At other times, the space used by the indexes might strike you as excessive.

Another good thing to keep in mind: you can have a maximum of 64 indexes per collection. Generally speaking, this is far more than you should need, but you could potentially hit this limit someday.

■ **Note** Adding an index increases query speed, but it reduces insertion or deletion speed. It's best to consider only adding indexes for collections where the number of reads is higher than the number of writes. When more writes occur than reads, indexes may even prove to be counterproductive.

Finally, all index information is stored in the system.indexes collection in your database. For example, you can run the db.system.indexes.find() command to take a quick peek at the indexes that have been stored so far. To see the indexes created for a specific collection, you can use the getIndexes command:

```
db.collection.getIndexes()
```

Implementing Geospatial Indexing

As Chapter 1 briefly mentioned, MongoDB has implemented *geospatial indexing* since version 1.4. This means that, in addition to normal indexes, MongoDB also supports geospatial indexes that are designed to work in an optimal way with location-based queries. For example, you can use this feature to find a number of closest known items to the user's current location. Or you might further refine your search to query for a specified number of restaurants near the current location. This type of query can be particularly helpful if you are designing an application where you want to find the closest available branch office to a given customer's ZIP code.

A document for which you want to add geospatial information must contain either a subobject or an array whose first element specifies the object type, followed by the item's longitude and latitude, as in the following example:

```
> db.restaurants.insert({name: "Kimono", loc: { type: "Point",
coordinates: [ 52.370451, 5.217497] } } )
```

Note that the type parameter can be used to specify the document's object type, which can be a Point, a LineString or a Polygon. As can be expected, the Point type is used to specify that the item (in this case, a restaurant) is located at exactly the spot given, thus requiring exactly two values, the longitute and latitude. The LineString type can be used to specify that the item extends along a specific line (say, a street), and thus requires a beginning and end point, as in the following example:

```
> db.streets.insert( {name: "Westblaak", loc: { type: "LineString",
coordinates: [ [52.36881, 4.890286],[52.368762, 4.890021] ] } } )
```

The Polygon type can be used to specify a (nondefault) shape (say, a shopping area). When using this type, you need to ensure that the first and last points are identical, to close the loop. Also, the point coordinates are to be provided as an array within an array, as in the following example:

```
> db.stores.insert( {name: "SuperMall", loc: { type: "Polygon", coordinates:
[ [ [52.146917, 5.374337], [52.146966, 5.375471], [52.146722, 5.375085],
[52.146744, 5.37437], [52.146917, 5.374337] ] ] } } )
```

In most cases, the Point type will be appropriate.

Once this geospatial information is added to a document, you can create the index (or even create the index beforehand, of course) and give the ensureIndex() function the 2dsphere parameter:

```
> db.restaurants.ensureIndex( { loc: "2dsphere" } )
```

> ■ **Note** The `ensureIndex()` function is used to add a custom index. Don't worry about the syntax of this function yet—you will learn how to use `ensureIndex()` in depth in the next chapter.

The `2dsphere` parameter tells `ensureIndex()` that it's indexing a coordinate or some other form of two-dimensional information on an Earth-like sphere. By default, `ensureindex()` assumes that a latitude/longitude key is given, and it uses a range of -180 to 180. However, you can overwrite these values using the `min` and `max` parameters:

```
> db.restaurants.ensureIndex( { loc: "2dsphere" }, { min : -500 , max : 500 } )
```

You can also expand your geospatial indexes by using *secondary key* values (also known as *compound keys*). This structure can be useful when you intend to query on multiple values, such as a location (geospatial information) and a category (sort ascending):

```
> db.restaurants.ensureIndex( { loc: "2dsphere", category: 1 } )
```

> ■ **Note** At this time, the geospatial implementation is based on the idea that the world is a perfect sphere. Thus, each degree of latitude and longitude is exactly 111km (69 miles) in length. However, this is only true exactly at the equator; the further you move away from the equator, the smaller each degree of longitude becomes, approaching zero at the poles.

Querying Geospatial Information

In this chapter, we are concerned primarily with two things: how to model the data and how a database works in the background of an application. That said, manipulating geospatial information is increasingly important in a wide variety of applications, so we'll take a few moments to explain how to leverage geospatial information in a MongoDB database.

Before getting started, a mild word of caution. If you are completely new to MongoDB and haven't had the opportunity to work with (geospatial) indexed data in the past, this section may seem a little overwhelming at first. Not to worry, however; you can safely skip it for now and come back to it later if you wish to. The examples given serve to show you a practical example of how (and why) to use geospatial indexing, making it easier to comprehend. With that out of the way, and if you are feeling brave, read on.

Once you've added data to your collection, and once the index has been created, you can do a geospatial query. For example, let's look at a few lines of simple yet powerful code that demonstrate how to use geospatial indexing.

Begin by starting up your MongoDB shell and selecting a database with the use function. In this case, the database is named restaurants:

```
> use restaurants
```

Once you've selected the database, you can define a few documents that contain geospatial information, and then insert them into the places collection (remember: you do not need to create the collection beforehand):

```
> db.restaurants.insert( { name: "Kimono", loc: { type: "Point",
coordinates: [ 52.370451, 5.217497] } } )

> db.restaurants.insert( {name: "Shabu Shabu", loc: { type: "Point",
coordinates: [51.915288, 4.472786] } } )

> db.restaurants.insert( {name: "Tokyo Cafe", loc: { type: "Point",
coordinates: [52.368736, 4.890530] } } )
```

After you add the data, you need to tell the MongoDB shell to create an index based on the location information that was specified in the loc key, as in this example:

```
> db.restaurants.ensureIndex ( { loc: "2dsphere" } )
```

Once the index has been created, you can start searching for your documents. Begin by searching on an exact value (so far this is a "normal" query; it has nothing to do with the geospatial information at this point):

```
> db.restaurants.find( { loc : [52,5] } )
>
```

The preceding search returns no results. This is because the query is *too* specific. A better approach in this case would be to search for documents that contain information *near* a given value. You can accomplish this using the $near operator. Note that this requires the type operator to be specified, as in the following example:

```
> db.restaurants.find( { loc : { $geoNear : { $geometry : { type : "Point",
coordinates: [52.338433, 5.513629] } } } } )
```

This produces the following output:

```
{
  "_id" : ObjectId("51ace0f380523d89efd199ac"),
  "name" : "Kimono",
  "loc" : {
    "type" : "Point",
    "coordinates" : [ 52.370451, 5.217497 ]
  }
}
```

```
{
  "_id" : ObjectId("51ace13380523d89efd199ae"),
  "name" : "Tokyo Cafe",
  "loc" : {
    "type" : "Point",
    "coordinates" : [ 52.368736, 4.89053 ]
  }
}
{
  "_id" : ObjectId("51ace11b80523d89efd199ad"),
  "name" : "Shabu Shabu",
  "loc" : {
    "type" : "Point",
    "coordinates" : [ 51.915288, 4.472786 ]
  }
}
```

Although this set of results certainly looks better, there's still one problem: all of the documents are returned! When used without any additional operators, $near returns the first 100 entries and sorts them based on their distance from the given coordinates. Now, while we can choose to limit our results to say, the first two items (or two hundred, if we want) using the limit function, even better would be to limit the results to those within a given range.

This can be achieved by appending the $maxDistance operator. Using this operator you can tell MongoDB to return only those results falling within a maximum distance (measured in meters) from the given point, as in the following example and its output:

```
> db.retaurants.find( { loc : { $geoNear : { $geometry : { type : "Point",
coordinates: [52.338433, 5.513629] }, $maxDistance : 40000 } } } )
{
  "_id" : ObjectId("51ace0f380523d89efd199ac"),
  "name" : "Kimono",
  "loc" : {
    "type" : "Point",
    "coordinates" : [ 52.370451, 5.217497 ]
  }
}
```

As you can see, this returns only a single result: a restaurant located within 40 kilometers (or, roughly 25 miles) from the starting point.

■ **Note** There is a direct correlation between the number of results returned and the time a given query takes to execute.

In addition to the $geoNear operator, MongoDB also includes a $geoWithin operator. You use this operator to find items in a particular shape. At this time, you can find items located in a $box, $polygon, $center and $centerSphere shape, where $box represents a rectangle, $polygon represents a specific shape of your choosing, $center represents a circle, and $centerSphere defines a circle on a sphere. Let's look at a couple of additional examples that illustrate how to use these shapes.

■ **Note**   With version 2.4 of MongoDB the $within operator was deprecated and replaced by $geoWithin. This operator does not strictly require a geospatial indexing. Also, unlike the $near operator, $geoWithin does not sort the returned results, improving their performance.

To use the $box shape, you first need to specify the lower-left, followed by the upper-right coordinates of the box, as in the following example:

```
> db.restaurants.find( { loc: { $geoWithin : { $box : [ [52.368549,
4.890238], [52.368849, 4.89094] ] } } } )
```

Similarly, to find items within a specific polygon form, you need to specify the coordinates of your points as a set of nested arrays. Again note that the first and last coordinates must be identical to close the shape properly, as shown in the following example:

```
> db.restaurants.find( { loc :
  { $geoWithin :
    { $geometry :
      { type : "Polygon" ,
        coordinates : [ [
          [52.368739, 4.890203], [52.368872, 4.890477], [52.368726, 4.890793],
          [52.368608, 4.89049], [52.368739, 4.890203]
        ] ]
      }
    }
  } )
```

The code to find items in a basic $circle shape is quite simple. In this case, you need to specify the center of the circle and its radius, measured in the units used by the coordinate system, before executing the find() function:

```
> db.restaurants.find( { loc: { $geoWithin : { $center : [ [52.370524,
5.217682], 10] } } } )
```

Note that ever since MongoDB version 2.2.3, the $center operator can be used without having a geospatial index in place. However, it is recommended to create one to improve performance.

Finally, to find items located within a circular shape on a sphere (say, our planet) you can use the $centerSphere operator. This operator is similar to $center, like so:

```
> db.restaurants.find( { loc: { $geoWithin : { $centerSphere : [ [52.370524,
5.217682], 10] } } } )
```

By default, the find() function is ideal for running queries. However, MongoDB also provides the geoNear() function, which works like the find() function, but also displays the distance from the specified point for each item in the results. The geoNear() function also includes some additional diagnostics. The following example uses the geoNear() function to find the two closest results to the specified position:

```
> db.runCommand( { geoNear : "restaurants", near : { type : "Point",
coordinates: [52.338433, 5.513629] }, spherical : true})
```

It returns the following results:

```
{
  "ns" : "stores.restaurants",
  "results" : [
    {
      "dis" : 33155.517810497055,
      "obj" : {
        "_id" : ObjectId("51ace0f380523d89efd199ac"),
        "name" : "Kimono",
        "loc" : {
          "type" : "Point",
          "coordinates" : [
            52.370451,
            5.217497
          ]
        }
      }
    },
    {
      "dis" : 69443.96264213261,
      "obj" : {
        "_id" : ObjectId("51ace13380523d89efd199ae"),
        "name" : "Tokyo Cafe",
        "loc" : {
          "type" : "Point",
          "coordinates" : [
            52.368736,
            4.89053
          ]
        }
      }
    },
```

```
{
    "dis" : 125006.87383713324,
    "obj" : {
        "_id" : ObjectId("51ace11b80523d89efd199ad"),
        "name" : "Shabu Shabu",
        "loc" : {
            "type" : "Point",
            "coordinates" : [
                51.915288,
                4.472786
            ]
        }
    }
}
],
"stats" : {
    "time" : 6,
    "nscanned" : 3,
    "avgDistance" : 75868.7847632543,
    "maxDistance" : 125006.87383713324
},
"ok" : 1
}
```

That completes our introduction to geospatial information for now; however, you'll see a few more examples that show you how to leverage geospatial functions in this book's upcoming chapters.

Using MongoDB in the Real World

Now that you have MongoDB and its associated plug-ins installed, and you have gained an understanding of the data model, it's time to get to work. In the next five chapters of the book, you will learn how to build, query, and otherwise manipulate a variety of sample MongoDB databases (see Table 3-1 for a quick view of the topics to come). Each chapter will stick primarily to using a single database that is unique to that chapter; we took this approach to make it easier to read this book in a modular fashion.

Table 3-1. *MongoDB Sample Databases Covered in This Book*

Chapter	Database Name	Topic
4	Library	Working with data and indexes
5	Test	GridFS
6	Contacts	PHP and MongoDB
7	Inventory	Python and MongoDB
8	Test	Advanced Queries

Summary

In this chapter, we looked at what's happening in the background of your database. We also explored the primary concepts of collections and documents in more depth; and we covered the datatypes supported in MongoDB, as well as how to embed and reference data.

Next, we examined what indexes do, including when and why they should be used (or not).

We also touched on the concepts of geospatial indexing. For example, we covered how geospatial data can be stored; we also explained how you can search for such data using either the regular find() function or the more geospatially based geoNear database command.

In the next chapter, we'll take a closer look at how the MongoDB shell works, including which functions can be used to insert, find, update, or delete your data. We will also explore how conditional operators can help you with all of these functions.

CHAPTER 4

Working with Data

In the previous chapter, you learned how the database works on the backend, what indexes are, how to use a database to quickly find the data you are looking for, and what the structure of a document looks like. You also saw a brief example that illustrated how to add data and find it again using the MongoDB shell. In this chapter, we will focus more on working with data from your shell.

We will use one database (named library) throughout this chapter, and we will perform actions such as adding data, searching data, modifying data, deleting data, and creating indexes. We'll also look at how to navigate the database using various commands, as well as what DBRef is and what it does. If you have followed the instructions in the previous chapters to set up the MongoDB software, you can follow the examples in this chapter to get used to the interface. Along the way, you will also attain a solid understanding of which commands can be used for what kind of operations.

Navigating Your Databases

The first thing you need to know is how to navigate your databases and collections. With traditional SQL databases, the first thing you would need to do is to create an actual database; however, as you probably remember from the previous chapters, this is not required with MongoDB because the program creates the database and underlying collection for you automatically the moment you store data in it.

To switch to an existing database or create a new one, you can use the use function in the shell, followed by the name of the database you would like to use, whether it exists or not. This snippet shows how to use the library database:

```
> use library
Switched to db library
```

The mere act of invoking the use function, followed by the database's name, sets your db (database) global variable to library. Doing this means that all the commands you pass down into the shell will automatically assume they need to be executed on the library database until you reset this variable to another database.

Viewing Available Databases and Collections

MongoDB automatically assumes a database needs to be created the moment you save data to it. It is also case-sensitive. For these reasons, it can be quite tricky to ensure that you're working in the correct database. Therefore, it's best to view a list of all current databases available to MongoDB prior to switching to one, in case you forgot the database's name or its exact spelling. You can do this using the show dbs function:

```
> show dbs
admin
local
```

Note that this function will only show a database that already exists. At this stage, the database does not contain any data yet, so nothing else will be listed. If you want to view all available collections for your current database, you can use the show collections function:

```
> show collections
system.indexes
```

Note that the system.indexes collection is created automatically the moment data is saved. This collection contains an index based on the _id key value from the document just inserted; it also includes any custom-created indexes that you've defined.

■ **Tip**   To view the database you are currently working in, simply type **db** into the MongoDB shell.

Inserting Data into Collections

One of the most frequently used pieces of functionality you will want to learn about is how to insert data into your collection. All data is stored in BSON format (which is both compact and reasonably fast to scan), so you will need to insert the data in BSON format as well. You can do this in several ways. For example, you can define it first, and then save it in the collection using the insert function, or you can type the document while using the insert function on the fly:

```
> document = ( { "Type" : "Book", "Title" : "Definitive Guide to MongoDB 2nd ed.,
The", "ISBN" : "978-1-4302-5821-6", "Publisher" : "Apress", "Author": [
"Hows, David", "Plugge, Eelco", "Membrey, Peter", "Hawkins, Tim" ] } )
```

■ **Note**   When you define a variable in the shell (for example, document = ({ ... })), the contents of the variable will be printed out immediately.

```
> db.media.insert(document)
```

Line breaks can also be used while typing in the shell. This can be convenient if you are writing a rather lengthy document, as in this example:

```
> document = ( { "Type" : "Book",
..."Title" : "Definitive Guide to MongoDB 2nd ed., The",
..."ISBN" : "978-1-4302-5821-6",
..."Publisher" : "Apress",
..."Author" : ["Hows, David", Plugge, Eelco", "Membrey, Peter"," "Hawkins, Tim"]
...} )
```

```
> db.media.insert(document)
```

As mentioned, the other option is to insert your data directly through the shell, without defining the document first. You can do this by invoking the insert function immediately, followed by the document's contents:

```
> db.media.insert( { "Type" : "CD", "Artist" : "Nirvana", "Title" :
"Nevermind" })
```

Or you can insert the data while using line breaks, as before. For example, you can expand the preceding example by adding an array of tracks to it. Pay close attention to how the commas and brackets are used in the following example:

```
> db.media.insert( { "Type" : "CD",
..."Artist" : "Nirvana",
..."Title" : "Nevermind",
... "Tracklist" : [
... {
... "Track" : "1",
... "Title" : "Smells Like Teen Spirit",
... "Length" : "5:02"
... },
... {
... "Track" : "2",
... "Title" : "In Bloom",
... "Length" : "4:15"
... }
... ]
...}
... )
```

As you can see, inserting data through the Mongo shell is straightforward.

The process of inserting data is extremely flexible, but you must adhere to some rules when doing so. For example, the names of the keys while inserting documents have the following limitations:

- The $ character must not be the first character in the key name. Example: $tags

- The period [.] character must not appear anywhere in the key name. Example: ta.gs

- The name _id is reserved for use as a primary key ID; although it is not recommended, it can store anything unique as a value, such as a string or an integer.

Similarly, some restrictions apply when creating a collection. For example, the name of a collection must adhere to the following rules:

- The collection's name cannot exceed 128 characters.

- An empty string (" ") cannot be used as a collection name.

- The collection's name must start with either a letter or an underscore.

- The collection name system is reserved for MongoDB and cannot be used.

- The collection's name cannot contain the "\0" null character.

Querying for Data

You've seen how to switch to your database and how to insert data; next, you will learn how to query for data in your collection. Let's build on the preceding example and look at all the possible ways to get a good clear view of your data in a given collection.

■ **Note** When querying your data, you have an extraordinary range of options, operators, expressions, filters, and so on available to you. We will spend the next few sections reviewing these options.

The find() function provides the easiest way to retrieve data from multiple documents within one of your collections. This function is one that you will be using often.

Let's assume that you have inserted the preceding two examples into a collection called media in the library database. If you were to use a simple find() function on this collection, you would get all of the documents you've added so far printed out for you:

```
> db.media.find()
{ "_id" : "ObjectId("4c1a8a56c603000000007ecb")", "Type" : "Book", "Title" :
"Definitive Guide to MongoDB 2nd ed., The", "ISBN" : "978-1-4302-5821-6",
"Publisher" :
"Apress", "Author" : ["Hows, David ", "Plugge, Eelco", "Membrey, Peter",
"Hawkins, Tim"]}

{ "_id" : "ObjectId("4c1a86bb2955000000004076")", "Type" : "CD", "Artist" :
"Nirvana", "Title" : "Nevermind", "Tracklist" : [
    {
        "Track" : "1",
            "Title" : "Smells Like Teen Spirit",
            "Length" : "5:02"
    },
    {
        "Track" : "2",
        "Title" : "In Bloom",
        "Length" : "4:15"
    }
] }
```

This is simple stuff, but typically you would not want to retrieve all the information from all the documents in your collection. Instead, you probably want to retrieve a certain type of document. For example, you might want to return all the CDs from Nirvana. If so, you can specify that only the desired information is requested and returned:

```
> db.media.find ( { Artist : "Nirvana" } )
{ "_id" : "ObjectId("4c1a86bb2955000000004076")", "Type" : "CD", "Artist" :
 "Nirvana", "Title" : "Nevermind", "Tracklist" : [
    {
        "Track" : "1",
        "Title" : "Smells Like Teen Spirit",
        "Length" : "5:02"
    },
    {
        "Track" : "2",
        "Title" : "In Bloom",
        "Length" : "4:15"
    }
] }
```

Okay, so this looks much better! You don't have to see all the information from all the other items you've added to your collection, only the information that interests you. However, what if you're still not satisfied with the results returned? For example, assume you want to get a list back that shows only the titles of the CDs you have by Nirvana, ignoring any other information, such as track lists. You can do this by inserting an additional parameter into your query that specifies the name of the key that you want to return, followed by a 1:

```
> db.media.find ( {Artist : "Nirvana"}, {Title: 1} )
{ "_id" : ObjectId("4c1a86bb2955000000004076"), "Title" : "Nevermind" }
```

Inserting the { Title : 1 } information specifies that only the information from the title field should be returned. The results are sorted and presented to you in ascending order.

▓ **Note**   The ascending order is based upon the insertion order of the document.

You can also accomplish the opposite: inserting { Type : 0 } retrieves a list of all items you have stored from Nirvana, showing all information except for the Type field.

▓ **Note**   The _id field will by default remain visible, unless you explicitly ask it not to show itself.

Take a moment to run the revised query with the { Title : 1 } insertion; no unnecessary information is returned at all. This saves you time because you see only the information you want. It also spares your database the time required to return unnecessary information.

Using the Dot Notation

When you start working with more complex document structures such as documents containing arrays or embedded objects, you can begin using other methods for querying information from those objects as well. For example, assume you want to find all CDs that contain a specific song you like. The following code executes a more detailed query:

```
> db.media.find( { "Tracklist.Title" : "In Bloom" } )
{ "_id" : "ObjectId("4c1a86bb2955000000004076"), "Type" : "CD", "Artist" :
"Nirvana", "Title" : "Nevermind", "Tracklist" : [
    {
        "Track" : "1",
        "Title" : "Smells Like Teen Spirit",
        "Length" : "5:02"
    },
```

```
    {
        "Track" : "2",
        "Title" : "In Bloom",
        "Length" : "4:15"
    }
] }
```

Using a period [.] after the key's name tells your find function to look for information embedded in your documents. Things are a little simpler when working with arrays. For example, you can execute the following query if you want to find a list of books written by Peter Membrey:

> db.media.find({ "Author" : "Membrey, Peter" })
```
{ "_id" : "ObjectId("4c1a8a56c603000000007ecb")", "Type" : "Book", "Title" :
"Definitive Guide to MongoDB 2nd ed., The", "ISBN" : "978-1-4302-5821-6",
"Publisher" :
"Apress", "Author" : ["Hows, David ", "Plugge, Eelco", "Membrey, Peter",
"Hawkins, Tim"] }
```

However, the following command will not match any documents, even though it might appear identical to the earlier track list query:

> db.media.find ({ "Tracklist" : {"Track" : "1" }})

Subobjects must match exactly; therefore, the preceding query would only match a document that contains no other information, such as Track.Title:

```
{"Type" : "CD",
"Artist" : "Nirvana"
"Title" : "Nevermind",
"Tracklist" : [
    {
        "Track" : "1",
    },
    {
        "Track" : "2",
        "Title" : "In Bloom",
        "Length" : "4:15"
    }
]
}
```

Using the Sort, Limit, and Skip Functions

MongoDB includes several functions that you can use for more precise control over your queries. We'll cover how to use the sort, limit, and skip functions in this section.

You can use the sort function to sort the results returned from a query. You can sort the results in ascending or descending order using 1 or -1, respectively. The function itself is analogous to the ORDER BY statement in SQL, and it uses the key's name and sorting method as criteria, as in this example:

```
> db.media.find().sort( { Title: 1 })
```

This example sorts the results based on the Title key's value in ascending order. This is the default sorting order when no parameters are specified. You would add the -1 flag to sort in descending order.

▨ **Note**   If you specify a key for sorting that does not exist, the values will be returned in their ascending insertion order.

You can use the limit() function to specify the maximum number of results returned. This function requires only one parameter: the number of the desired results returned. When you specify '0', all results will be returned. The following example returns only the first ten items in your media collection:

```
> db.media.find().limit( 10 )
```

Another thing you might want to do is skip the first *n* documents in a collection. The following example skips the first twenty documents in your media collection:

```
> db.media.find().skip( 20 )
```

As you probably surmised, this command returns all documents within your collection, except for the first twenty it finds. Remember: it finds documents in the order they were inserted.

MongoDB wouldn't be particularly powerful if it weren't able to combine these commands. However, practically any function can be combined and used in conjunction with any other function. The following example limits the results by skipping a few and then sorts the results in descending order:

```
> db.media.find().sort ( { Title : -1 } ).limit ( 10 ).skip ( 20 )
```

You might use this example if you want to implement paging in your application. As you might have guessed, this command wouldn't return any results in the media collection created so far, because the collection contains fewer documents than were skipped in this example.

You can use the following shortcut in the find() function to skip and limit your results: find ({}, {}, 10, 20). Here, you limit the results to 10 and skip the first 20 documents.

Working with Capped Collections, Natural Order, and $natural

There are some additional concepts and features you should be aware of when sorting queries with MongoDB, including capped collections, natural order, and $natural. We'll explain what all of these terms mean and how you can leverage them in your sorts in this section.

The *natural order* is the database's native ordering method for objects within a (normal) collection. So, when you query for items in a collection, the items are returned by default in the *forward natural order*. This is usually identical to the order in which items were inserted; however, that is not guaranteed to be the case, as data can move when it no longer fits on its old location after being modified.

A *capped collection* is a collection in your database where the natural order is guaranteed to be the order in which the documents were inserted. Guaranteeing that the natural order will always match the insertion order can be particularly useful when you're querying data and need to be absolutely certain that the results returned are already sorted based on their order of insertion.

Capped collections have another great benefit: they are a fixed size. Once a capped collection is full, the oldest data will be purged, and newer data will be added at the end, ensuring that the natural order follows the order in which the records were inserted. This type of collection can be used for logging and auto-archiving data.

Unlike a standard collection, a capped collection must be created explicitly, using the createCollection function. You must also supply parameters that specify the size (in bytes) of the collection you want to add. For example, imagine you want to create a capped collection named audit with a maximum size of 20480 bytes:

```
> db.createCollection("audit", {capped:true, size:20480})
{ "ok" : 1 }
```

Given that a capped collection guarantees that the natural order matches the insertion order, you don't need to include any special parameters or any other special commands or functions when querying the data either, except of course when you want to reverse the default results. This is where the $natural parameter comes in. For example, assume you want to find the ten *most recent* entries from your capped collection that lists failed login attempts. You could use the $natural parameter to find this information:

```
> db.audit.find().sort( { $natural: -1 } ).limit ( 10 )
```

■ **Note**   Documents already added to a capped collection can be updated, but they must
not grow in size. The update will fail if they do. Deleting documents from a capped
collection is also not possible; instead, the entire collection must be dropped and re-created
if you want to do this. You will learn more about dropping a collection later in this chapter.

You can also limit the number of items added into a capped collection using the `max:`
parameter when you create the collection. However, you must take care to ensure that
there is enough space in the collection for the number of items you want to add. If the
collection becomes full before the number of items has been reached, the oldest item in
the collection will be removed. The MongoDB shell includes a utility that lets you see the
amount of space used by an existing collection, whether it's capped or uncapped. You
invoke this utility using the `validate()` function. This can be particularly useful if you
want to estimate how large a collection might become.

As stated previously, you can use the `max:` parameter to cap the number of items that
can be inserted into a collection, as in this example:

```
> db.createCollection("audit100", { capped:true, size:20480, max: 100})
{ "ok" : 1 }
```

Next, use the `validate()` function to check the size of the collection:

```
> db.audit100.validate()
{
    "ns" : "media.audit100",
    "result" : "
        validate
        capped:1 max:100
        firstExtent:0:54000 ns:media.audit100
        lastExtent:0:54000 ns:media.audit100
        # extents:1
        datasize?:0 nrecords?:0 lastExtentSize:20736
        padding:1
        first extent:
        loc:0:54000 xnext:null xprev:null
        nsdiag:media.audit100
        size:20736 firstRecord:null lastRecord:null
        capped outOfOrder:0 (OK)
        0 objects found, nobj:0
        0 bytes data w/headers
        0 bytes data wout/headers
        deletedList: 1100000000000000000
        deleted: n: 2 size: 20560
        nIndexes:0
```

```
",
"ok" : 1,
"valid" : true,
"lastExtentSize" : 20736
}
```

The resulting output shows that the table (named audit100) is a capped collection with a maximum of 100 items to be added, and it currently contains zero items.

Retrieving a Single Document

So far we've only looked at examples that show how to retrieve multiple documents. If you want to receive only one result, however, querying for all documents—which is what you generally do when executing a find() function—would be a waste of CPU time and memory. For this case, you can use the findOne() function to retrieve a single item from your collection. Overall, the result is identical to what occurs when you append the limit(1) function, but why make it harder on yourself than you should?

The syntax of the findOne() function is identical to the syntax of the find() function:

> **db.media.findOne()**

It's generally advised to use the findOne() function if you expect only one result.

Using the Aggregation Commands

MongoDB comes with a nice set of aggregation commands. You might not see their significance at first, but once you get the hang of them, you will see that the aggregation commands form an extremely powerful set of tools. For instance, you might use them to get an overview of some basic statistics about your database. In this section, we will take a closer look at how to use three of the functions from the available aggregate commands: count, distinct, and group.

In addition to these three basic aggregation commands, MongoDB also includes an aggregation framework. This powerful feature will allow you to calculate aggregated values without needing to use the—often overly complex—map/reduce framework. The aggregation framework will be discussed in Chapter 5.

Returning the Number of Documents with count()

The count() function returns the number of documents in the specified collection. So far we've added a number of documents in the *media* collection. The count() function can tell you exactly how many:

> **db.media.count()**
2

You can also perform additional filtering by combining count() with conditional operators, as shown here:

```
> db.media.find( { Publisher : "Apress", Type: "Book" } ).count()
1
```

This example returns only the number of documents added in the collection that are published by Apress and of the type Book. Note that the count() function ignores a skip() or limit() parameter by default. To ensure that your query doesn't skip these parameters and that your count results will match the limit and/or skip parameters, use count(true):

```
> db.media.find( { Publisher: "Apress", Type: "Book" }).skip ( 2 ) .count
(true)
0
```

Retrieving Unique Values with distinct()

The preceding example shows a great way to retrieve the total number of documents from a specific publisher. However, this approach is definitely not precise. After all, if you own more than one book with the same title (for instance, the hardcopy and the e-book), then you would technically have just one book. This is where distinct() can help you: it will only return unique values.

For the sake of completeness, you can add an additional item to the collection. This item carries the same title, but has a different ISBN number:

```
> document = ( { "Type" : "Book","Title" : "Definitive Guide to MongoDB 2nd
ed., The", ISBN:
"978-1-4302-5821-6", "Publisher" : "Apress", "Author" :
["Hows, David","Membrey, Peter","Plugge, Eelco","Hawkins, Tim"] } )
> db.media.insert (document)
```

At this point, you should have two books in the database with identical titles. When using the distinct() function on the titles in this collection, you will get a total of two unique items. However, the titles of the two books are unique, so they will be grouped into one item. The other result will be the title of the album "Nevermind":

```
> db.media.distinct( "Title")
[ "Definitive Guide to MongoDB, The", "Nevermind" ]
```

Similarly, you will get two results if you query for a list of unique ISBN numbers:

```
> db.media.distinct ("ISBN")
[ "1-4302-3051-7", "987-4302-3051-9" ]
```

The distinct() function also takes nested keys when querying; for instance, this command will give you a list of unique titles of your CDs:

```
> db.media.distinct ("Tracklist.Title")
[ "In Bloom", "Smells Like Teen Spirit" ]
```

Grouping Your Results

Last but not least, you can group your results. MongoDB's group() function is similar to SQL's GROUP BY function, although the syntax is a little different. The purpose of the command is to return an array of grouped items. The group() function takes three parameters: key, initial, and reduce.

The key parameter specifies which results you want to group. For example, assume you want to group results by Title. The initial parameter lets you provide a base for each grouped result (that is, the base number of items to start off with). By default, you want to leave this parameter at zero if you want an exact number returned. The reduce parameter groups all similar items together. Reduce takes two arguments: the current document being iterated over and the aggregation counter object. These arguments are called items and prev in the example that follows. Essentially, the reduce parameter adds a 1 to the sum of every item it encounters that matches a title it has already found.

The group() function is ideal when you're looking for a *tagcloud* kind of function. For example, assume you want to obtain a list of all unique titles of *any* type of item in your collection. Additionally, assume you want to group them together if any doubles are found, based on the title:

```
> db.media.group (
{
    key: {Title : true},
    initial: {Total : 0},
    reduce : function (items,prev)
    {
        prev.Total += 13
    }
}
)

[
    {
        "Title" : "Nevermind",
        "Total" : 1
    },
    {
        "Title" : "Definitive Guide to MongoDB, The",
        "Total" : 2
    }
]
```

In addition to the key, initial, and reduce parameters, you can specify three more optional parameters:

- keyf: You can use this parameter to replace the key parameter if you do not wish to group the results on an existing key in your documents. Instead, you would group them using another function you design that specifies how to do grouping.

- cond: You can use this parameter to specify an additional statement that must be true before a document will be grouped. You can use this much as you use the find() query to search for documents in your collection. If this parameter isn't set (the default), then all documents in the collection will be checked.

- finalize: You can use this parameter to specify a function you want to execute before the final results are returned. For instance, you might calculate an average or perform a count and include this information in the results.

■ **Note**   The group() function does not currently work in sharded environments. For these, you should use the mapreduce() function instead. Also, the resulting output cannot contain more than 10,000 keys in all with the group() function, or an exception will be raised. This too, can be bypassed by using mapreduce().

Working with Conditional Operators

MongoDB supports a large set of conditional operators to better filter your results. The following sections provide an overview of these operators, including some basic examples that show you how to use them. Before walking through these examples, however, you should add a few more items to the database; doing so will let you see the effects of these operators more plainly:

```
dvd = ( { "Type" : "DVD", "Title" : "Matrix, The", "Released" : 1999,
    "Cast" : ["Keanu Reeves","Carrie-Anne Moss","Laurence Fishburne","Hugo
    Weaving","Gloria Foster","Joe Pantoliano"] } )
{
        "Type" : "DVD",
        "Title" : "Matrix, The",
        "Released" : 1999,
        "Cast" : [
                "Keanu Reeves",
                "Carrie-Anne Moss",
                "Laurence Fishburne",
```

```
                "Hugo Weaving",
                "Gloria Foster",
                "Joe Pantoliano"
        ]
}
> db.media.insert(dvd)

> dvd = ( { "Type" : "DVD", Title : "Blade Runner", Released : 1982 } )
{ "Type" : "DVD", "Title" : "Blade Runner", "Released" : 1982 }
> db.media.insert(dvd)

> dvd = ( { "Type" : "DVD", Title : "Toy Story 3", Released : 2010 } )
{ "Type" : "DVD", "Title" : "Toy Story 3", "Released" : 2010 }
> db.media.insert(dvd)
```

Performing Greater-Than and Less-Than Comparisons

You can use the following special parameters to perform greater-than and less-than comparisons in queries: $gt, $lt, $gte, and $lte. In this section, we'll look at how to use each of these parameters.

The first one we'll cover is the $gt (greater than) parameter. You can use this to specify that a certain integer should be greater than a specified value in order to be returned:

```
> db.media.find ( { Released : {$gt : 2000} }, { "Cast" : 0 } )
{ "_id" : ObjectId("4c4369a3c603000000007ed3"), "Type" : "DVD", "Title" :
"Toy Story 3", "Released" : 2010 }
```

Note that the year 2000 itself will not be included in the preceding query. For that, you use the $gte (greater than or equal to) parameter:

```
> db.media.find ( { Released : {$gte : 1999 } }, { "Cast" : 0 } )
{ "_id" : ObjectId("4c43694bc603000000007ed1"), "Type" : "DVD", "Title" :
"Matrix, The", "Released" : 1999 }
{ "_id" : ObjectId("4c4369a3c603000000007ed3"), "Type" : "DVD", "Title" :
"Toy Story 3", "Released" : 2010 }
```

Likewise, you can use the $lt (less than) parameter to find items in your collection that predate the year 1999:

```
> db.media.find ( { Released : {$lt : 1999 } }, { "Cast" : 0 } )
{ "_id" : ObjectId("4c436969c603000000007ed2"), "Type" : "DVD", "Title" :
"Blade Runner", "Released" : 1982 }
```

You can also get a list of items older than or equal to the year 1999 by using the $lte (less than or equal to) parameter:

```
> db.media.find( {Released : {$lte: 1999}}, { "Cast" : 0 })
{ "_id" : ObjectId("4c43694bc603000000007ed1"), "Type" : "DVD", "Title" :
"Matrix, The", "Released" : 1999 }
{ "_id" : ObjectId("4c436969c603000000007ed2"), "Type" : "DVD", "Title" :
"Blade Runner", "Released" : 1982 }
```

You can also combine these parameters to specify a range:

```
> db.media.find( {Released : {$gte: 1990, $lt : 2010}}, { "Cast" : 0 })
{ "_id" : ObjectId("4c43694bc603000000007ed1"), "Type" : "DVD", "Title" :
"Matrix, The", "Released" : 1999 }
```

These parameters might strike you as relatively simple to use; however, you will be using them a lot when querying for a specific range of data.

Retrieving All Documents but Those Specified

You can use the $ne (not equals) parameter to retrieve every document in your collection, except for the ones that match certain criteria. For example, you can use this snippet to obtain a list of all books where the author is not Eelco Plugge:

```
> db.media.find( { Type : "Book", Author: {$ne : "Plugge, Eelco"}})
```

Specifying an Array of Matches

You can use the $in operator to specify an array of possible matches. The SQL equivalent is the IN operator.

You can use the following snippet to retrieve data from the media collection using the $in operator:

```
> db.media.find( {Released : {$in : [1999,2008,2009] } }, { "Cast" : 0 } )
{ "_id" : ObjectId("4c43694bc603000000007ed1"), "Type" : "DVD", "Title" :
"Matrix, The", "Released" : 1999 }
```

This example returns only one item, because only one item matches the release year of 1999, and there are no matches for the years 2008 and 2009.

Finding a Value Not in an Array

The $nin operator functions similarly to the $in operator, except that it searches for the objects where the specified field does *not* have a value in the specified array:

```
> db.media.find( {Released : {$nin : [1999,2008,2009] },Type : "DVD" },
{ "Cast" : 0 } )
{ "_id" : ObjectId("4c436969c603000000007ed2"), "Type" : "DVD", "Title" :
"Blade Runner", "Released" : 1982 }
{ "_id" : ObjectId("4c4369a3c603000000007ed3"), "Type" : "DVD", "Title" :
"Toy Story 3", "Released" : 2010 }
```

Matching All Attributes in a Document

The $all operator also works similarly to the $in operator. However, $all requires that all attributes match in the documents, whereas only one attribute must match for the $in operator. Let's look at an example that illustrates these differences. First, here's an example that uses $in:

```
> db.media.find ( { Released : {$in : ["2010","2009"] } }, { "Cast" : 0 } )
{ "_id" : ObjectId("4c4369a3c603000000007ed3"), "Type" : "DVD", "Title" :
"Toy Story 3", "Released" : 2010 }
```

One document is returned for the $in operator because there's a match for 2010, but not for 2009. However, the $all parameter doesn't return any results, because there are no matching documents with 2009 in the value:

```
> db.media.find ( { Released : {$all : ["2010","2009"] } }, { "Cast" : 0 } )
```

Searching for Multiple Expressions in a Document

You can use the $or operator to search for multiple expressions in a single query, where only one criterion needs to match to return a given document. Unlike the $in operator, $or allows you to specify both the key and the value, rather than only the value:

```
> db.media.find({ $or : [ { "Title" : "Toy Story 3" }, { "ISBN" :
"987-1-4302-3051-9" } ] } )
{ "_id" : ObjectId("4c5fc7d8db290000000067c5"), "Type" : "Book", "Title" :
"Definitive Guide to MongoDB, The", "ISBN" : "987-1-4302-3051-9",
"Publisher" : "Apress", "Author" : ["Hows, David", "Membrey, Peter",
"Plugge, Eelco",
"Hawkins, Tim" ] }
{ "_id" : ObjectId("4c5fc943db290000000067ca"), "Type" : "DVD", "Title" :
"Toy Story 3", "Released" : 2010 }
```

It's also possible to combine the $or operator with another query parameter. This will restrict the returned documents to only those that match the first query (mandatory), and then either of the two key/value pairs specified at the $or operator, as in this example:

```
> db.media.find({ "Type" : "DVD", $or : [ { "Title" : "Toy Story 3" }, {
"ISBN" : "987-1-4302-3051-9" } ] })
{ "_id" : ObjectId("4c5fc943db290000000067ca"), "Type" : "DVD", "Title" :
"Toy Story 3", "Released" : 2010 }
```

You could say that the $or operator allows you to perform two queries at the same time, combining the results of two otherwise unrelated queries.

Retrieving a Document with $slice

You can use the $slice operator to retrieve a document that includes a specific area from an array in that document. This can be particularly useful if you want to limit a certain set of items added to save bandwidth. The operator also lets you retrieve the results *n* items per page, a feature generally known as *paging*.

In theory, the $slice operator combines the capabilities of the limit() and skip() functions; however, limit() and skip()do not work on an array, whereas $slice does. The operator takes two parameters; the first indicates the total number of items to be returned. The second parameter is optional; if used, it ensures that the *first* parameter defines the offset, while the *second* defines the limit. The limit parameter can also indicate a negative condition.

The following example limits the items from the Cast list to the first three items:

```
> db.media.find({"Title" : "Matrix, The"}, {"Cast" : {$slice: 3}})
{ "_id" : ObjectId("4c5fcd3edb290000000067cb"), "Type" : "DVD", "Title" :
"Matrix, The", "Released" : 1999, "Cast" : [ "Keanu Reeves", "Carrie-Anne
Moss", "Laurence Fishburne" ] }
```

You can also get only the last three items by making the integer negative:

```
> db.media.find({"Title" : "Matrix, The"}, {"Cast" : {$slice: -3}})
{ "_id" : ObjectId("4c5fcd3edb290000000067cb"), "Type" : "DVD", "Title" :
"Matrix, The", "Released" : 1999, "Cast" : [ "Hugo Weaving", "Gloria
Foster",
"Joe Pantoliano" ] }
```

Or you can skip the first two items and limit the results to three from that particular point (pay careful attention to the brackets):

```
> db.media.find({"Title" : "Matrix, The"}, {"Cast" : {$slice: [2,3] }})
{ "_id" : ObjectId("4c5fcd3edb290000000067cb"), "Type" : "DVD", "Title" :
"Matrix, The", "Released" : 1999, "Cast" : [ "Laurence Fishburne", "Hugo
Weaving", "Gloria Foster" ] }
```

Finally, when specifying a negative integer, you can skip to the last five items and limit the results to four, as in this example:

```
> db.media.find({"Title" : "Matrix, The"}, {"Cast" : {$slice: [-5,4] }})
{ "_id" : ObjectId("4c5fcd3edb290000000067cb"), "Type" : "DVD", "Title" :
"Matrix, The", "Released" : 1999, "Cast" : [ "Carrie-Anne Moss","Laurence
Fishburne","Hugo Weaving","Gloria Foster"] }
```

■ **Note** With version 2.4 MongoDB also introduced the $slice operator for $push operations, allowing you to limit the number of array elements when appending values to an array. This operator is discussed later in this chapter. Do not confuse the two, however.

Searching for Odd/Even Integers

The $mod operator lets you search for specific data that consists of an even or uneven number. This works because the operator takes the modulus of 2 and checks for a remainder of 0, thereby providing even-numbered results only.

For example, the following code returns any item in the collection that has an even-numbered integer set to its Released field:

```
> db.media.find ( { Released : { $mod: [2,0] } }, {"Cast" : 0 } )
{ "_id" : ObjectId("4c45b5c18e0f0000000062aa"), "Type" : "DVD", "Title" :
"Blade Runner", "Released" : 1982 }
{ "_id" : ObjectId("4c45b5df8e0f0000000062ab"), "Type" : "DVD", "Title" :
"Toy Story 3", "Released" : 2010 }
```

Likewise, you can find any documents containing an uneven value in the Released field by changing the parameters in $mod, as follows:

```
> db.media.find ( { Released : { $mod: [2,1] } }, { "Cast" : 0 } )
{ "_id" : ObjectId("4c45b5b38e0f0000000062a9"), "Type" : "DVD", "Title" :
"Matrix, The", "Released" : 1999 }
```

■ **Note** The $mod operator only works on integer values, not on strings that contain a numbered value. For example, you can't use the operator on { Released : "2010" }, because it's in quotes and therefore a string.

Filtering Results with $size

The $size operator lets you filter your results to match an array with the specified number of elements in it. For example, you might use this operator to do a search for those CDs that have exactly two songs on them:

```
> db.media.find ( { Tracklist : {$size : 2} } )
{ "_id" : ObjectId("4c1a86bb2955000000004076"), "Type" : "CD", "Artist" :
"Nirvana", "Title" : "Nevermind", "Tracklist" : [
        {
                "Track" : "1",
                "Title" : "Smells Like Teen Spirit",
                "Lenght" : "5:02"
        },
        {
                "Track" : "2",
                "Title" : "In Bloom",
                "Length" : "4:15"
        }
] }
```

▨ **Note** You cannot use the $size operator to find a range of sizes. For example, you cannot use it to find arrays with more than one element in them.

Returning a Specific Field Object

The $exists operator allows you to return a specific object if a specified field is either missing or found. The following example returns all items in the collection with a key named Author:

```
> db.media.find ( { Author : {$exists : true } } )
```

Similarly, if you invoke this operator with a value of false, then all documents that don't have a key named Author will be returned:

```
> db.media.find ( { Author : {$exists : false } } )
```

▨ **Warning** Currently, the $exists operator is unable to use an index; therefore, using it requires a full table scan.

Matching Results Based on the BSON Type

The $type operator lets you match results based on their BSON type. For instance, the following snippet lets you find all items that have a track list of the type Embedded Object (that is, it contains a list of information):

```
> db.media.find ( { Tracklist: { $type : 3 } } )
{ "_id" : ObjectId("4c1a86bb2955000000004076"), "Type" : "CD", "Artist" :
"Nirvana", "Title" : "Nevermind", "Tracklist" : [
        {
                "Track" : "1",
                "Title" : "Smells Like Teen Spirit",
                "Lenght" : "5:02"
        },
        {
                "Track" : "2",
                "Title" : "In Bloom",
                "Length" : "4:15"
        }
] }
```

The known data types are defined in Table 4-1.

Table 4-1. *Known BSON Types and Codes*

Code	Data Type	Code	Data Type
–1	MiniKey	11	Regular Expression
1	Double	13	JavaScript Code
2	Character string (UTF8)	14	Symbol
3	Embedded object	15	JavaScript Code with scope
4	Embedded array	16	32-bit integer
5	Binary Data	17	Timestamp
7	Object ID	18	64-bit integer
8	Boolean type	127	MaxKey
9	Date type	255	MinKey
10	Null type		

Matching an Entire Array

If you want to match an entire array within a document, you can use the $elemMatch operator. This is particularly useful if you have multiple documents within your collection, some of which have some of the same information. This can make a default query incapable of finding the exact document you are looking for. This is because the standard query syntax doesn't restrict itself to a single document within an array.

Let's look at an example that illustrates this principle. For this to work, we need to add another document to the collection, one that has an identical item in it, but is otherwise different. Specifically, we'll add another CD from Nirvana that happens to have the same track on it as the aforementioned CD ("Smells Like Teen Spirit"). However, on this version of the CD, the song is track 5, not track 1:

```
{
        "Type" : "CD",
        "Artist" : "Nirvana",
        "Title" : "Nirvana",
        "Tracklist" : [
                {
                        "Track" : "1",
                        "Title" : "You know you're right",
                        "Length" : "3:38"
                },
                {
                        "Track" : "5",
                        "Title" : "Smells like teen spirit",
                        "Length" : "5:02"
                }
        ]
}
```

```
> nirvana = ( { "Type" : "CD", "Artist" : "Nirvana", "Title" : "Nirvana",
"Tracklist" : [ { "Track" : "1", "Title" : "You Know You're Right", "Length"
: "3:38"}, {"Track" : "5", "Title" : "Smells Like Teen Spirit", "Length" :
"5:02" } ] } )
```

```
> db.media.insert(nirvana)
```

If you want to search for an album from Nirvana that has the song "Smells Like Teen Spirit" as Track 1 on the CD, you might think that the following query would do the job:

```
> db.media.find ( { "Tracklist.Title" : "Smells Like Teen Spirit",
"Tracklist.Track" : "1" } )
```

Unfortunately, the preceding query will return both documents. The reason for this is that both documents have a track with the title called "Smells Like Teen Spirit" and both have a track number 1. If you want to match an entire document within the array, you can use $elemMatch, as in this example:

```
> db.media.find ( { Tracklist: { "$elemMatch" : { Title:
"Smells like teen spirit", Track : "1" } } } )

{ "_id" : ObjectId("4c1a86bb2955000000004076"), "Type" : "CD", "Artist" :
"Nirvana", "Title" : "Nevermind", "Tracklist" : [
        {
                "Track" : "1",
                "Title" : "Smells Like Teen Spirit",
                "Lenght" : "5:02"
        },
        {
                "Track" : "2",
                "Title" : "In Bloom",
                "Length" : "4:15"
        }
] }
```

This query gave the desired result and only returned the first document.

$not (meta-operator)

You can use the $not meta-operator to negate any check performed by a standard operator. The following example returns all documents in your collection, except for the one seen in the $elemMatch example:

```
> db.media.find ( { Tracklist : { $not : { "$elemMatch" : { Title:
"Smells Like Teen Spirit", "Track" : "1" } } } } )
```

Specifying Additional Query Expressions

Apart from the structured query syntax you've seen so far, you can also specify additional query expressions in JavaScript. The big advantage of this is that JavaScript is extremely flexible and allows you to do tons of additional things. The downside of using JavaScript is that it's a tad slower than the native operators baked into MongoDB.

For example, assume you want to search for a DVD within your collection that is older than 1995. All of the following code examples would return this information:

```
db.media.find ( { "Type" : "DVD", "Released" : { $lt : 1995 } } )

db.media.find ( { "Type" : "DVD", $where: "this.Released < 1995" } )

db.media.find ("this.Released < 1995")

f = function() { return this.Released < 1995 }
db.media.find(f)
```

And *that's* how flexible MongoDB is! Using these operators should enable you to find just about anything throughout your collections.

Leveraging Regular Expressions

Regular expressions are another powerful tool you can use to query information. *Regular expressions—regex*, for short—are special text strings that you can use to describe your search pattern. These work much like wildcards, but they are far more powerful and flexible.

MongoDB allows you to use these regular expressions when searching for data in your collections; however, it will attempt to use an index whenever possible for simple prefix queries.

The following example uses regex in a query to find all items in the media collection that start with the word "Matrix":

```
> db.media.find ( { Title : /Matrix*/i } )
```

Using regular expressions from MongoDB can make your life much simpler, so we'd recommend exploring this feature in greater detail as time permits or your circumstances can benefit from it.

Updating Data

So far you've learned how to insert and query for data in your database. Next, you'll learn how to update that data. MongoDB supports quite a few update operators that you'll learn how to use in the following sections.

Updating with update()

MongoDB comes with the update() function for performing updates to your data. The update() function takes three primary arguments: criteria, objNew and options.

The `criteria` argument lets you specify the query that selects the record you want to update. You use the `objNew` argument to specify the updated information; or you can use an operator to do this for you. The `options` argument lets you specify your options when updating the document, and has two possible values: `upsert` and `multi`. The `upsert` option lets you specify whether the update should be an *upsert*—that is, it tells MongoDB to update the record if it exists, and create it if it doesn't. Finally, the `multi` option lets you specify whether all matching documents should be updated or just the first one (the default action).

The following simple example uses the `update()` function without any fancy operators:

```
> db.media.update( { "Title" : "Matrix, The"}, {"Type" : "DVD", "Title" :
"Matrix, The", "Released" : 1999, "Genre" : "Action"}, { upsert: true} )
```

This example overwrites the document in the collection and saves it with the new values specified. Note that any fields that you leave out are removed (the document is basically being rewritten). Because the `upsert` argument is specified as `true`, any fields that do not exist yet will be added (the `Genre` key/value pair, in this case).

In case there happen to be multiple documents matching the criteria and you wish to upsert them all, the `upsert` and `multi` options can be added while using the `$set` modifier operator as shown here:

```
> db.media.update( { "Title" : "Matrix, The"}, {$set: {"Type" : "DVD",
"Title" :
"Matrix, The", "Released" : 1999, "Genre" : "Action"} }, {upsert: true,
multi: true} )
```

■ **Note**   An `upsert` tells the database to "update a record if a document is present or to insert the record if it isn't."

Implementing an Upsert with the save( ) Command

You can also perform an upsert with the `save()` command. To do this, you need to specify the `_id` value; you can have this value added automatically or specify it manually yourself. If you do not specify the `_id` value, the `save()` command will assume it's an insert and simply add the document into your collection.

The main benefit of using the `save()` command is that you do not need to specify that the upsert method should be used in conjunction with the `update()` command. Thus, the `save()` command gives you a quicker way to upsert data. In practice, the `save()` and `update()` commands look similar:

```
> db.media.update( { "Title" : "Matrix, The"}, {"Type" : "DVD", "Title" :
"Matrix, The", "Released" : "1999", "Genre" : "Action"}, { upsert: true} )
```

```
> db.media.save( { "Title" : "Matrix, The"}, {"Type" : "DVD", "Title" :
"Matrix, The", "Released" : "1999", "Genre" : "Action"})
```

Obviously, this example assumes that the Title value acts as the id field.

Updating Information Automatically

You can use the modifier operations to update information quickly and simply in your documents, but without needing to type everything in manually. For example, you might use these operations to increase a number or to remove an element from an array.

We'll be exploring these operators next, providing practical examples that show you how to use them.

Incrementing a Value with $inc

The $inc operator enables you to perform an (atomic) update on a key to increase the value by the given increment, assuming that the field exists. If the field doesn't exist, it will be created. To see this in action, begin by adding another document to the collection:

```
> manga = ( { "Type" : "Manga", "Title" : "One Piece", "Volumes" : 612,
"Read" : 520 } )
{
        "Type" : "Manga",
        "Title" : "One Piece",
        "Volumes" : "612",
        "Read" : "520"
}
> db.media.insert(manga)
```

Now you're ready to update the document. For example, assume you've read another four volumes of the One Piece manga, and you want to increment the number of Read volumes in the document. The following example shows you how to do this:

```
> db.media.update ( { "Title" : "One Piece"}, {$inc: {"Read" : 4} } )
> db.media.find ( { "Title" : "One Piece" } )
{
        "Type" : "Manga",
        "Title" : "One Piece ",
        "Volumes" : "612",
        "Read" : "524"
}
```

Setting a Field's Value

You can use the $set operator to set a field's value to one you specify. This goes for any datatype, as in the following example:

```
> db.media.update ( { "Title" : "Matrix, The" }, {$set : { Genre :
"Sci-Fi" } } )
```

This snippet would update the genre in the document created earlier, setting it to Sci-Fi instead.

Deleting a Specified Field

The $unset operator lets you delete a given field, as in this example:

```
> db.media.update ( {"Title": "Matrix, The"}, {$unset : { "Genre" : 1 } } )
```

This snippet would delete the Genre key and its value from the document.

Appending a Value to a Specified Field

The $push operator allows you to append a value to a specified field. If the field is an existing array, then the value will be added. If the field doesn't exist yet, then the field will be set to the array value. If the field exists, but it isn't an array, then an error condition will be raised.

Begin by adding another author to your entry in the collection:

```
> db.media.update ( {"ISBN" : "978-1-4302-5821-6"}, {$push: { Author :
"Griffin,
Stewie"} } )
```

The next snippet raises an error message because the Title field is not an array:

```
> db.media.update ( {"ISBN" : "978-1-4302-5821-6"}, {$push: { Title :
"This isn't an array"} } )
Cannot apply $push/$pushAll modifier to non-array
```

The following example shows how the document looks in the meantime:

```
> db.media.find ( { "ISBN" : "978-1-4302-5821-6" } )
{
    "Author" :
    [
        "Hows, David",
        "Membrey, Peter",
        "Plugge, Eelco",
        "Griffin, Stewie",
    ],
```

```
    "ISBN" : "978-1-4302-5821-6",
    "Publisher" : "Apress",
    "Title" : "Definitive Guide to MongoDB 2nd ed., The",
    "Type" : "Book",
    "_id" : ObjectId("4c436231c603000000007ed0")
}
```

Specifying Multiple Values in an Array

When working with arrays, the $push operator will append the value specified to the given array, expanding the data stored within the given element. If you wish to add several separate values to the given array, you can use the optional $each modifier as in this example:

```
> db.media.update( { "ISBN" : "978-1-4302-5821-6" }, { $push: { Author : {
$each: ["Griffin, Peter", "Griffin, Brian"] } } } )
{
    "Author" :
    [
        "Hows, David",
        "Membrey, Peter",
        "Plugge, Eelco",
        "Hawkins, Tim",
        "Griffin, Stewie",
        "Griffin, Peter",
        "Griffin, Brian"
    ],
    "ISBN" : "978-1-4302-5821-6",
    "Publisher" : "Apress",
    "Title" : "Definitive Guide to MongoDB 2nd ed., The",
    "Type" : "Book",
    "_id" : ObjectId("4c436231c603000000007ed0")
}
```

Optionally, you can use the $slice operator when using $each. This allows you to limit the number of elements within an array during a $push operation. $slice takes either a negative number or zero. Using a negative number ensures that only the last *n* elements will be kept within the array, whereas using zero would empty the array. Note that the $slice operator has to be the first modifier to the $push operator in order to function as such:

```
> db.media.update( { "ISBN" : "978-1-4302-5821-6" }, { $push: { Author : {
$each: ["Griffin, Meg", "Griffin, Louis"], $slice: -2 } } } )
{
    "Author" :
    [
        "Griffin, Meg",
        "Griffin, Louis"
    ],
    "ISBN" : "978-1-4302-5821-6",
    "Publisher" : "Apress",
    "Title" : "Definitive Guide to MongoDB 2nd ed., The",
    "Type" : "Book",
    "_id" : ObjectId("4c436231c603000000007ed0")
}
```

As you can see, the $slice operator ensured that not only were the two new values pushed, the data kept within the array was also limited to the value specified (two). The $slice operator can be a valuable tool when working with fixed-sized arrays.

Adding Data to an Array with $addToSet

The $addToSet operator is another command that lets you add data to an array. However, this operator only adds the data to the array if the data is not already there. In this way, $addToSet is unlike $push. By default, the $addToSet operator takes one argument. However, you can use the $each operator to specify additional arguments when using t$addToSet. The following snippet adds the author Griffin, Brian into the authors array because it isn't there yet:

```
> db.media.update( { "ISBN" : "1-4302-3051-7" }, {$addToSet : { Author :
"Griffin, Brian" } } )
```

Executing the snippet again won't change anything because the author is already in the array.

To add more than one value, however, you should take a different approach and use the $each operator, as well:

```
> db.media.update( { "ISBN" : "1-4302-3051-7" }, {$addToSet : { Author :
{ $each : ["Griffin, Brian","Griffin, Meg"] } } } )
```

At this point, our document, which once looked tidy and trustworthy, has been transformed into something like this:

```
{
    "Author" :
    [
        "Hows, David",
        "Membrey, Peter",
        "Plugge, Eelco",
        "Hawkins, Tim",
        "Griffin, Stewie",
        "Griffin, Peter",
        "Griffin, Brian",
        "Griffin, Louis",
        "Griffin, Meg"
    ],
    "ISBN" : "1-4302-3051-7",
    "Publisher" : "Apress",
    "Title" : "Definitive Guide to MongoDB, The",
    "Type" : "Book",
    "_id" : ObjectId("4c436231c603000000007ed0")
}
```

Removing Elements from an Array

MongoDB also includes several methods that let you remove elements from an array, including $pop, $pull, $pullAll. In the sections that follow, you'll learn how to use each of these methods for removing elements from an array.

The $pop operator lets you remove a single element from an array. This operator lets you remove the first or last value in the array, depending on the parameter you pass down with it. For example, the following snippet removes the last element from the array:

> **db.media.update({ "ISBN" : "1-4302-3051-7" }, {$pop : {Author : 1 } })**

In this case, the $pop operator will *pop* Meg's name off the list of authors. Passing down a negative number would remove the first element from the array. The following example removes Peter Membrey's name from the list of authors:

> **db.media.update({ "ISBN" : "1-4302-3051-7" }, {$pop : {Author : -1 } })**

■ **Note**   Specifying a value of -2 or 1000 wouldn't change which element gets removed. Any negative number would remove the first element, while any positive number would remove the last element. Using the number 0 removes the last element from the array.

Removing Each Occurrence of a Specified Value

The $pull operator lets you remove each occurrence of a specified value from an array.
This can be particularly useful if you have multiple elements with the same value in your
array. Let's begin this example by using the $push parameter to add Stewie back to the list
of authors:

```
> db.media.update ( {"ISBN" : "1-4302-3051-7"}, {$push: { Author :
"Griffin, Stewie"} } )
```

Stewie will be in and out of the database a couple more times as we walk through this
book's examples. You can remove all occurrences of this author in the document with the
following code:

```
> db.media.update ( {"ISBN" : "1-4302-3051-7"}, {$pull : { Author :
"Griffin,
Stewie" } } )
```

Removing Multiple Elements from an Array

You can also remove multiple elements with different values from an array. The $pullAll
operator enables you to accomplish this. The $pullAll operator takes an array with all
the elements you want to remove, as in the following example:

```
> db.media.update( { "ISBN" : "1-4302-3051-7"}, {$pullAll : { Author :
["Griffin, Louis","Griffin, Peter","Griffin, Brian"] } } )
```

The field from which you remove the elements (Author in the preceding example)
needs to be an array. If it isn't, you'll receive an error message.

Specifying the Position of a Matched Array

You can use the $ operator in your queries to specify the position of the matched array
item in your query. You can use this operator for data manipulation after finding an array
member. For instance, assume you've added another track to your track list, but you
accidently made a typo when entering the track number:

```
> db.media.update( { "Title" : "Nirvana" }, {$addToSet : { Tracklist :
{"Track" : 2,"Title": "Been a Son", "Length":"2:23"} } } )

{
    "Artist" : "Nirvana",
    "Title" : "Nirvana",
```

```
    "Tracklist" : [
        {
                "Track" : "1",
                "Title" : "You Know You're Right",
                "Length" : "3:38"
        },
        {

                "Track" : "5",
                "Title" : "Smells Like Teen Spirit",
                "Length" : "5:02"
        },
        {

                "Track" : 2,
                "Title" : "Been a Son",
                "Length" : "2:23"
        }
    ],
    "Type" : "CD",
    "_id" : ObjectId("4c443ad6c603000000007ed5")
}
```

It so happens you know that the track number of the most recent item should be 3 rather than 2. You can use the $inc method in conjunction with the $ operator to increase the value from 2 to 3, as in this example:

```
> db.media.update( { "Tracklist.Title" : "Been a son"},
{$inc:{"Tracklist.$.Track" : 1} } )
```

Note that only the first item it matches will be updated. Thus, if there are two identical elements in the comments array, only the first element will be increased.

Atomic Operations

MongoDB supports atomic operations executed against single documents. An *atomic operation* is a set of operations that can be combined in such a way that the set of operations appears to be merely one single operation to the rest of the system. This set of operations will have either a positive or a negative outcome as the final result.

You can call a set of operations an atomic operation if it meets the following pair of conditions:

1. No other process knows about the changes being made until the entire set of operations has completed.

2. If one of the operations fails, the entire set of operations (the entire atomic operation) will fail, resulting in a full rollback, where the data is restored to its state prior to running the atomic operation.

A standard behavior when executing atomic operations is that the data will be *locked* and therefore unable to be reached by other queries. However, MongoDB does not support locking or complex transactions for a number of reasons:

- In sharded environments (see Chapter 12 for more information on such environments), distributed locks can be expensive and slow. MongoDB's goal is to be lightweight and fast, so expensive and slow goes against the principle.

- MongoDB developers don't like the idea of deadlocks. In their view, it's preferable for a system to be simple and predictable instead.

- MongoDB is designed to work well for real-time problems. When an operation is executed that locks large amounts of data, it would also stop some smaller light queries for an extended period of time. Again, this goes against the MongoDB goal of speed.

MongoDB includes several update operators (as noted previously), all of which can atomically update an element:

- $set: Sets a particular value.

- $unset: Removes a particular value.

- $inc: Increments a particular value by a certain amount.

- $push: Appends a value to an array.

- $pull: Removes one or more values from an existing array.

- $pullAll: Removes several values from an existing array.

Using the Update if Current Method

Another strategy that atomic update uses is the *update-if-current* method. This method takes the following three steps:

1. It fetches the object from the document.

2. It modifies the object locally (with any of the previously mentioned operations, or a combination of them).

3. It sends an update request to update the object to the new value, in case the current value still matches the old value fetched.

You can review the result of the operation to see how many documents were updated and if there were any errors. Consider the following update:

```
> db.media.update( { "Tracklist.Title" : "Been a son"},
{$inc:{"Tracklist.$.Track" : 1} } )
```

When you issue this command you should see the following result:

```
WriteResult({ "nMatched" : 1, "nUpserted" : 0, "nModified" : 1 })
```

We can see from this result, that our update matched one document and modified one document.

In this example, you incremented `Tracklist.Track` using the track list title as an identifier. But now consider what happens if the track list data is changed by another user using the same method while MongoDB was modifying your data. Because `Tracklist.Title` remains the same, you might assume (incorrectly) that you are updating the original data, when in fact you are overwriting the changes.

This is known as *the ABA problem*. This scenario might seem unlikely, but in a multi-user environment, where many applications are working on data at the same time, this can be a significant problem.

To avoid this problem, you can do one of the following:

- Use the entire object in the update's query expression, instead of just the _id and `comments.by` field.

- Use $set to set the field you care about. If other fields have changed, they won't be affected by this.

- Put a version variable in the object and increment it on each update.

- When possible, use a $ operator instead of an update-if-current sequence of operations.

■ **Note** MongoDB does not support updating multiple documents atomically in a single operation. Instead, you can use nested objects, which effectively make them one document for atomic purposes.

Modifying and Returning a Document Atomically

The `findAndModify` command also allows you to perform an atomic update on a document. This command modifies the document and returns it. The command takes three main operators: `<query>`, which you use to specify the document you're executing it against; `<sort>`, used to sort the matching documents when multiple match, and `<operations>`, which you use to specify what needs to be done.

Now let's look at a handful of examples that illustrate how to use this command. The first example finds the document you're searching for and removes it once it is found:

```
> db.media.findAndModify( { "Title" : "One Piece",sort:{"Title": -1},
remove:
true} )
{
        "_id" : ObjectId("4c445218c603000000007ede"),
        "Type" : "Manga",
        "Title" : "One Piece",
        "Volumes" : 612,
        "Read" : 524
}
```

This code returned the document it found matching the criteria. In this case, it found and removed the first item it found with the title "One Piece." If you execute a find() function now, you will see that the document is no longer within the collection.

The next example modifies the document rather than removing it:

```
> db.media.findAndModify( { query: { "ISBN" : "987-1-4302-3051-9" }, sort:
{"Title":-1}, update: {$set: {"Title" : " Different Title"} } } )
```

The preceding example updates the title from "Definitive Guide to MongoDB, The" to "Different Title"—and returns the old document (as it was before the update) to your shell. If you would rather see the results of the update on the document instead, you can add the new operator after your query:

```
> db.media.findAndModify( { query: { "ISBN" : "987-1-4302-3051-9" }, sort:
{"Title":-1}, update: {$set: {"Title" : " Different Title"} }, new:true } )
```

Note that you can use any modifier operation with this command, not just $set.

Renaming a Collection

It might happen that you discover you have named a collection incorrectly, but you've already inserted some data into it. This might make it troublesome to remove and read the data again from scratch.

Instead, you can use the renameCollection() function to rename your existing collection. The following example shows you how to use this simple and straightforward command:

```
> db.media.renameCollection("newname")
{ "ok" : 1 }
```

If the command executes successfully, an OK will be returned. If it fails, however (if the collection doesn't exist, for example), then the following message is returned:

```
{ "errmsg" : "assertion: source namespace does not exist", "ok" : 0 }
```

The renameCollection command doesn't take many parameters (unlike some commands you've seen so far); however, it can be quite useful in the right circumstances.

Removing Data

So far we've explored how to add, search for, and modify data. Next, we'll examine how to *remove* documents, entire collections, and the databases themselves.

Previously, you learned how to remove data from a specific document (using the $pop command, for instance). In this section, you will learn how to remove full documents and collections. Just as the insert() function is used for inserting and update() is used for modifying a document, remove() is used to remove a document.

To remove a single document from your collection, you need to specify the criteria you'll use to find the document. A good approach is to perform a find() first; this ensures that the criteria used are specific to your document. Once you are sure of the criterion, you can invoke the remove() function using that criterion as a parameter:

```
> db.newname.remove( { "Title" : "Different Title" } )
```

This statement removes the book added previously or any other item in your collection that has the same title. The fact this statement removes all books by that title is one reason why it's best to specify the item's _id value—it's always unique.

Or you can use the following snippet to remove all documents from the newname library (remember, we renamed the media collection this previously):

```
> db.newname.remove({})
```

▨ **Warning**   When removing a document, you need to remember that any reference to that document will remain within the database. For this reason, be sure you manually delete or update those references as well; otherwise, these references will return null when evaluated. Referencing will be discussed in the next section.

If you want to remove an entire collection, you can use the drop() function. The following snippet removes the entire newname collection, including all of its documents:

```
> db.newname.drop()
true
```

The drop() function returns either true or false, depending on whether the operation has completed successfully. Likewise, if you want to remove an entire database from MongoDB, you can use the dropDatabase() function, as in this example:

```
> db.dropDatabase()
{ "dropped" : "library", "ok" : 1 }
```

Note that this snippet will remove the database you are currently working in (again, be sure to check db to see which database is your current database).

Referencing a Database

At this point, you have an empty database again. You're also familiar with inserting various kinds of data into a collection. Now you're ready to take things a step further and learn about *database referencing*. As you've already seen, there are plenty of scenarios where embedding data into your document will suffice for your application (such as the track list or the list of authors in the book entry). However, sometimes you do need to reference information in another document. The following sections will explain how to go about doing so.

Just as with SQL, references between documents in MongoDB are resolved by performing additional queries on the server. MongoDB gives you two ways to accomplish this: referencing them manually or using the DBRef standard, which many drivers also support.

Referencing Data Manually

The simplest and most straightforward way to reference data is to do so manually. When referencing data manually, you store the value from the _id of the other document in your document, either through the full ID or through a simpler common term. Before proceeding with an example, let's add a new document and specify the publisher's information in it (pay close attention to the _id field:

```
> apress = ( { "_id" : "Apress", "Type" : "Technical Publisher", "Category"
:
["IT", "Software","Programming"] } )
{
        "_id" : "Apress",
        "Type" : "Technical Publisher",
        "Category" : [
                "IT",
                "Software",
                "Programming"
        ]
}
> db.publisherscollection.insert(apress)
```

Once you add the publisher's information, you're ready to add an actual document (for example, a book's information) into the media collection. The following example adds a document, specifying Apress as the name of the publisher:

```
> book = ( { "Type" : "Book", "Title" : "Definitive Guide to MongoDB 2nd
ed., The",
"ISBN" : "987-1-4302-5821-6", "Publisher" : "Apress","Author" : ["Hows,
David",""Plugge, Eelco","Membrey,Peter",Hawkins, Tim"] } )
{
        "Type" : "Book",
        "Title" : "Definitive Guide to MongoDB 2nd ed., The",
        "ISBN" : "987-1-4302-5821-6",
        "Publisher": "Apress",
        "Author" : [
                "Hows, David"
                "Membrey, Peter",
                "Plugge, Eelco",
                "Hawkins, Tim"
        ]
}
> db.media.insert(book)
```

All the information you need has been inserted into the publisherscollection and media collections, respectively. You can now start using the database reference. First, specify the document that contains the publisher's information to a variable:

```
> book = db.media.findOne()
{
        "_id" : ObjectId("4c458e848e0f00000000628e"),
        "Type" : "Book",
        "Title" : "Definitive Guide to MongoDB, The",
        "ISBN" : "987-1-4302-3051-9",
        "Publisher" : "Apress",
        "Author" : [
                "Hows, David"
                "Membrey, Peter",
                "Plugge, Eelco",
                "Hawkins, Tim"
        ]
}
```

To obtain the information itself, you combine the findOne function with some dot notation:

```
> db.publisherscollection.findOne( { _id : book.Publisher } )
{
        "_id" : "Apress",
        "Type" : "Technical Publisher",
        "Category" : [
                "IT",
                "Software",
                "Programming"
        ]
}
```

As this example illustrates, referencing data manually is straightforward and doesn't require much brainwork. Here, the _id in the documents placed in the users collection has been manually set and has not been generated by MongoDB (otherwise, the _id would be an object ID).

Referencing Data with DBRef

The DBRef standard provides a more formal specification for referencing data between documents. The main reason for using DBRef over a manual reference is that the collection can change from one document to the next. So, if your referenced collection will always be the same, the referencing data manually (as just described) is fine.

With DBRef, the database reference is stored as a standard embedded (JSON/BSON) object. Having a standard way to represent references means that drivers and data frameworks can add helper methods that manipulate the references in standard ways.

The syntax for adding a DBRef reference value looks like this:

```
{ $ref : <collectionname>, $id : <id value>[, $db : <database name>] }
```

Here, <collectionname> represents the name of the collection referenced (for example, publisherscollection); <id value> represents the value of the _id field for the object you are referencing; and the optional $db allows you to reference documents that are placed in other databases.

Let's look at another example using DBRef from scratch. Begin by emptying your two collections and adding a new document:

```
> db.publisherscollection.drop()
true
> db.media.drop()
true
> apress = ( { "Type" : "Technical Publisher", "Category" :
```

```
["IT","Software","Programming"] } )
{
        "Type" : "Technical Publisher",
        "Category" : [
                "IT",
                "Software",
                "Programming"
        ]
}
> db.publisherscollection.save(apress)
```

So far you've defined the variable apress and saved it using the save() function. Next, display the updated contents of the variable by typing in its name:

```
> apress
{
"Type" : "Technical Publisher",
"Category" : [
    "IT",
    "Software",
    "Programming"
],
"_id" : ObjectId("4c4597e98e0f000000006290")
}
```

So far you've defined the publisher and saved it to the publisherscollection collection. Now you're ready to add an item to the *media* collection that references the data:

```
> book = { "Type" : "Book", "Title" : "Definitive Guide to MongoDB 2nd ed.,
The",
"ISBN" : "978-1-4302-5821-6", "Author": ["Hows, David","Membrey,
Peter","Plugge,
Eelco","Hawkins, Tim"], Publisher : [ new DBRef ('publisherscollection',
apress._id) ] }

{
        "Type" : "Book",
        "Title" : "Definitive Guide to MongoDB 2nd ed., The",
        "ISBN" : "987-1-4302-5821-6",
        "Author" : [
                "Hows, David"
                "Membrey, Peter",
```

```
            "Plugge, Eelco",
            "Hawkins, Tim"

        ],
        "Publisher" : [
                DBRef("publishercollection", "Apress")
        ]
}
> db.media.save(book)
```

And that's it! Granted, the example looks a little less simple than the manual method of referencing data; however, it's a good alternative for cases where collections can change from one document to the next.

Implementing Index-Related Functions

In the previous chapter, you took a brief look at what indexes can do for your database. Now it's time to briefly learn how to create and use indexes. Indexing will be discussed in greater detail in Chapter 10, but for now let's look at the basics. MongoDB includes a fair number of functions available for maintaining your indexes; we'll begin by creating an index with the ensureIndex() function.

The ensureIndex() function takes at least one parameter, which is the name of a key in one of your documents that you will use to build the index. In the previous example, you added a document to the media collection that used the Title key. This collection would be well served by an index on this key.

■ **Tip** The rule of thumb in MongoDB is to create an index for the same sort of scenarios where you'd want to create one in MySQL.

You can create an index for this collection by invoking the following command:

```
> db.media.ensureIndex( { Title : 1 } )
```

This command ensures that an index will be created for all the Title values from all documents in the media collection. The :1 at the end of the line specifies the direction of the index: 1 stores the items in ascending order, whereas -1 stores them in descending order.

```
// Ensure ascending index
db.media.ensureIndex( { Title :1 } )

// Ensure descending index
db.media.ensureIndex( { Title :-1 } )
```

■ **Tip**   Searching through indexed information is fast. Searching for non-indexed information is slow, as each document needs to be checked to see if it's a match.

BSON allows you to store full arrays in a document; however, it would also be beneficial to be able to create an index on an embedded key. Luckily, the developers of MongoDB thought of this, too, and added support for this feature. Let's build on one of the earlier examples in this chapter, adding another document into the database that has embedded information:

```
> db.media.insert( { "Type" : "CD", "Artist" : "Nirvana","Title" :
"Nevermind", "Tracklist" : [ { "Track" : "1", "Title" : "Smells Like Teen
Spirit", "Length" : "5:02" }, {"Track" : "2","Title" : "In Bloom", "Length"
:
"4:15" } ] } )

{ "_id" : ObjectId("4c45aa2f8e0f000000006293"), "Type" : "CD", "Artist" :
"Nirvana", "Title" : "Nevermind", "Tracklist" : [
        {
                "Track" : "1",
                "Title" : "Smells Like Teen Spirit",
                "Length" : "5:02"
        },
        {
                "Track" : "2",
                "Title" : "In Bloom",
                "Length" : "4:15"
        }
] }
```

Next, you can create an index on the Title key for all entries in the track list:

```
> db.media.ensureIndex( { "Tracklist.Title" : 1 } )
```

The next time you perform a search for any of the titles in the collection—assuming they are nested under Tracklist—the titles will show up instantly. Next, you can take this concept one step further and use an entire (sub)document as a key, as in this example:

```
> db.media.ensureIndex( { "Tracklist" : 1 } )
```

This statement indexes each element of the array, which means you can now search for any object in the array. These types of keys are also known as *multi keys*. You can also create an index based on multiple keys in a set of documents. This process is known as *compound indexing*. The method you use to create a compound index is mostly the same; the difference is that you specify several keys instead of one, as in this example:

```
> db.media.ensureIndex({"Tracklist.Title": 1, "Tracklist.Length": -1})
```

The benefit of this approach is that you can make an index on multiple keys (as in the previous example, where you indexed an entire subdocument). Unlike the subdocument method, however, compound indexing lets you specify whether you want one of the two fields to be indexed in descending order. If you perform your index with the subdocument method, you are limited to ascending or descending order only. There is more on compound indexes in Chapter 10.

Surveying Index-Related Commands

So far you've taken a quick glance at one of the index-related commands, ensureIndex(). Without a doubt, this is the command you will primarily use to create your indexes. However, you might also find a pair of additional functions useful: hint() and min()/max(). You use these functions to query for data. We haven't covered them to this point because they won't function without a custom index. But now let's take a look at what they can do for you.

Forcing a Specified Index to Query Data

You can use the hint() function to force the use of a specified index when querying for data. The intended benefit of using this command is to improve the query performance. To see this principle in action, try performing a find with the hint() function without defining an index:

```
> db.media.find( { ISBN: " 978-1-4302-5821-6"} ) . hint ( { ISBN: -1 } )
error: { "$err" : "bad hint", "code" : 10113 }
```

If you create an index on ISBN numbers, this technique will be more successful. Note that the first command's background parameter ensures that the indexing is done on the background:

```
> db.media.ensureIndex({ISBN: 1}, {background: true});
> db.media.find( { ISBN: " 978-1-4302-5821-6"} ) . hint ( { ISBN: 1 } )

{ "_id" : ObjectId("4c45a5418e0f000000006291"), "Type" : "Book", "Title"
: "Definitive Guide to MongoDB, The", "ISBN" : " 978-1-4302-5821-6",
"Author" : ["Hows, David","Membrey, Peter", "Plugge, Eelco","Hawkins,Tim"],
"Publisher" : [
        {
                "$ref" : "publisherscollection",
                "$id" : ObjectId("4c4597e98e0f000000006290")
        }
] }
```

To confirm that the given index is being used, you can optionally add the explain() function, returning information about the query plan chosen. Here, the indexBounds value tells you about the index used:

```
> db.media.find( { ISBN: " 978-1-4302-5821-6"} ) . hint ( { ISBN: 1 }
).explain()
{
    "cursor" : "BtreeCursor ISBN_1",
    "isMultiKey" : false,
    "n" : 1,
    "nscannedObjects" : 1,
    "nscanned" : 1,
    "nscannedObjectsAllPlans" : 1,
    "nscannedAllPlans" : 1,
    "scanAndOrder" : false,
    "indexOnly" : false,
    "nYields" : 0,
    "nChunkSkips" : 0,
    "millis" : 0,
    "indexBounds" : {
        "ISBN" : [
            [
                {
                    "$minElement" : 1
                },
                {
                    "$maxElement" : 1
                }
            ]
        ]
    },
    "server" : "localhost:27017"
}
```

Constraining Query Matches

The min() and max() functions enable you to constrain query matches to only those that have index keys between the min and max keys specified. Therefore, you will need to have an index for the keys you are specifying. Also, you can either combine the two functions or use them separately. Let's begin by adding a few documents that enable you to take advantage of these functions. First, create an index on the Released field:

```
> db.media.insert( { "Type" : "DVD", "Title" : "Matrix, The", "Released" :
1999} )
> db.media.insert( { "Type" : "DVD", "Title" : "Blade Runner", "Released" :
1982 } )
> db.media.insert( { "Type" : "DVD", "Title" : "Toy Story 3", "Released" :
2010} )
> db.media.ensureIndex( { "Released": 1 } )
```

You can now use the max() and min() commands, as in this example:

```
> db.media.find() . min ( { Released: 1995 } ) . max ( { Released : 2005 } )
{ "_id" : ObjectId("4c45b5b38e0f0000000062a9"), "Type" : "DVD", "Title" :
"Matrix, The", "Released" : 1999 }
```

If no index is created, then an error message will be returned, saying that no index has been found for the specified key pattern. Obviously, you will need to define which index must be used with the hint() function:

```
> db.media.find() . min ( { Released: 1995 } ) .
max ( { Released : 2005 } ). hint ( { Released : 1 } )
{ "_id" : ObjectId("4c45b5b38e0f0000000062a9"), "Type" : "DVD", "Title" :
"Matrix, The", "Released" : 1999 }
```

■ **Note**   The min() value will be *included* in the results, whereas the max() value will be *excluded* from the results.

Generally speaking, it is recommended that you use $gt and $lt (greater than and less than, respectively) rather than min() and max() because $gt and $lt don't require an index. The min() and max() functions are used primarily for compound keys.

Summary

In this chapter, we've taken a look at the most commonly used commands and options that can be performed with the MongoDB shell to manipulate data. We also examined how to search for, add, modify, and delete data, and how to modify your collections and databases. Next, we took a quick look at atomic operations, how to use aggregation, and when to use operators such as $elemMatch. Finally, we explored how to create indexes and when to use them. We examined what indexes are used for, how you can drop them, how to search for your data using the indexes created, and how to check for running indexing operations.

In the next chapter, we'll look into the fundamentals of GridFS, including what it is, what it does, and how it can be used to your benefit.

CHAPTER 5

■ ■ ■

GridFS

We live in a world of high-definition video, 12MP cameras, and storage media that can hold 50GB of data on a disc the size of a CD-ROM. In that context, the 16MB limit for the maximum size of a MongoDB document might seem laughably inadequate. Indeed, you might wonder why MongoDB, which has been designed as a database for today's high-tech age, has such a seemingly strange limitation. The short answer is performance.

If data were stored in the document itself, it would obviously get very large, which in turn would make the data harder to work with. For example, pulling back the whole document would require loading the files in the document, as well. You could work around this issue, but you would still need to pull back the entire file whenever you accessed it, even if you only wanted a small section of it. You can't ask for a chunk of data in the middle of a document—it's an all-or-nothing proposition. Fortunately, MongoDB features a unique and somewhat elegant solution to this problem. MongoDB enables you to store large files quite easily, yet it also allows you to access parts of the file without retrieving the entire thing—all while maintaining high performance. It achieves this by leveraging a specification known as GridFS.

■ **Note**   One interesting thing about GridFS is that it isn't actually a software feature. For example, there isn't any special server-side code in MongoDB that manages GridFS. Instead, GridFS is a simple specification used by all of the supported drivers on MongoDB. The key benefit of such a specification is that files stored by one driver can be accessed by any other driver that follows the same convention.

This approach adheres closely to the MongoDB principle of keeping things simple. Because GridFS uses standard MongoDB features, it's easy to implement and work with the specification from the driver's point of view. It also means you can poke around by hand if you really want to, as to MongoDB files in the GridFS specification are just normal collections containing documents.

Filling in Some Background

Chapter 1 touched on the fact that we have been taught to use databases for even simple storage for many years. For example, the book one of us bought to help improve his PHP more than 15 years ago introduced MySQL in Chapter 3. Considering the complexity of SQL and databases in the real world (not to mention in theory), you might wonder why a book intended for beginners would practically start off with SQL. After all, it was a PHP book and not a MySQL book.

One thing most people don't appreciate until they try it is that reading and writing data directly to disk is hard. Some people don't agree with us on this point—after all, opening and reading files in Python might seem trivial. And it is: in simpler scenarios, working with files is rather painless when using PHP. If all you want to do is read in lines and process them, you're unlikely to have any trouble.

On the other hand, things become a lot harder if you want to search a file or store complicated or structured data. Even if you can work out how to do this and create a solution, your solution is unlikely to be faster or more efficient than relying on a database instead. Today's applications depend on finding and storing data quickly—and databases make this possible for those of us who can't or don't want to write such a system ourselves.

One area that is glossed over by many books is the storing of files. Most books that teach you to use a database to store your data also teach you to read and write to the filesystem instead when you need to store files. In some ways, this isn't usually a problem, because it's much easier to read and write simple files than to process what's in them. There are some issues, however. First, the developer must have permission to write those files in the first place, and that requires giving the web server permission to write to the local filesystem. This might not seem likely to pose a problem, but it gives system administrators nightmares—getting files onto a server is the first stage in being able to compromise it.

Databases can store binary files; typically, it's just not elegant for them to do so. MySQL has a special column type called BLOB. PostgreSQL requires special procedures to be followed to store such files—and the data isn't stored in the table itself. In other words, it's messy. These solutions are obviously bolt-ons. Thus, it's not surprising that people choose to write data to the disk instead. But that approach also has issues. Apart from the problems with security, it adds another directory that needs to be backed up, and you must also ensure that this information is replicated to all the appropriate servers. There are filesystems that provide the ability to write to disk and have that content fully replicated (including GFS); but these solutions are complex and add overhead; moreover, these features typically make your solution harder to maintain.

MongoDB, on the other hand, enforces a maximum document size of 16MB. This is more than enough for storing rich documents, and it might have sufficed a few years ago for storing many other types of files as well. However, this limit is wholly inadequate for today's environment.

Working with GridFS

Next, we'll take a brief look at how GridFS is implemented. As the MongoDB website points out, you do not need to understand or be aware of the underlying implementation of GridFS to use it. In fact, you can simply let the driver handle the heavy lifting for you. For the most part, the drivers that support GridFS implement file handling in a language-specific way. For example, the MongoDB driver for Python works in a manner that is wholly consistent with Python, as you'll see shortly. If the ins-and-outs of GridFS don't interest you, then just skip ahead to the next section. We promise you won't miss anything that enables you to use MongoDB effectively!

GridFS consists of two parts. More specifically, it consists of two collections. One collection holds the filename and related information such as size (called metadata), while the other collection holds the file data itself, usually in 256K chunks. The specification calls for these to be named files and chunks, respectively. By default, the files and chunks collections are created in the fs namespace, but this can be changed. The ability to change the default namespace is useful if you want to store different types of files. For example, you might want to keep image and movie files separate.

Getting Started with the Command-Line Tools

Now that we have some of the background out of the way, let's look at how to get started with GridFS by exploring the command-line tools available to leverage it. First, we will need a file to play with. To keep things simple, let's use the dictionary file. On Ubuntu, you can find this at /usr/share/dict/words. However, there are various levels of symbolic links, so you might want to run this command first:

```
root@core2:/usr/share/dict# cat words > /tmp/dictionary
```

■ **Note** In Ubuntu, you might need to use apt-get install wbritish to get the dictionary file installed.

This command copies all the contents of the file to a nice and simple path that you can use easily. Of course, you can use any file that you wish for this example; it doesn't need to be any particular size or type.

Rather than describe all the options you can use with, let's jump right in and start playing with some of the tool's features. This book assumes that you're running mongofiles on the same machine as MongoDB. If you're not, then you'll need to use the -h option to specify the host that MongoDB is running on. You'll learn about the other options available in the mongofiles command after putting it through its paces.

First, let's list all the files in the database. We're not expecting any files to be in there yet, but let's make sure. The list command lists the files in the database so far:

```
$ mongofiles list
connected to: 127.0.0.1
$
```

OK, so that probably wasn't very exciting. Keep in mind that mongofiles is a proof-of-concept tool; it's probably not a tool you will use much with your own applications. However, mongofiles is great for learning and testing. Once you create a file, you can use the tool to explore the files and chunks that are created.

Let's kick things up a notch and the put command to add the dictionary file created previously (remember: you can use any file that you like for this example):

```
$ mongofiles put /tmp/dictionary
connected to: 127.0.0.1
added file: { _id: ObjectId('51cb61b26487b3d8ce7af440'), filename: "/tmp/
dictionary", chunkSize: 262144, uploadDate: new Date(1372283314621), md5:
"40c0825855792bd20e8a2d515fe9c3e3", length: 4953699 }}}
done!
$
```

This example returns some useful information; however, let's double-check the information it shows by confirming that the file is there. Do so by rerunning the list command:

```
$ mongofiles list
connected to: 127.0.0.1
/tmp/dictionary 4953699
$
```

This example shows the dictionary file, along with its size. The information clearly comes from the files collection, but we're getting ahead of ourselves. Let's take a moment to step back and examine the output returned from the put command in this example.

Using the _id Key

As you know, each document in MongoDB includes a unique identifier stored in the _id key. Like MySQL's auto_increment field, the _id key is not of much direct interest, apart from the fact that it allows you to pick out a specific file.

Working with Filenames

The output from the put command also shows a Filename key, which itself needs a little explanation. Generally, you will want to keep this field unique to help prevent major confusion; however, that's not entirely necessary. In fact, if you run the put command again, you'll end up with two documents that look identical. In this case, the files and metadata are identical, apart from the _id key. You might be surprised by this and wonder why MongoDB doesn't update the file that exists rather than create a new one. The reason is that there could be many cases where you would have filenames that are identical. For example, if you built a system to store student assignments, then chances are pretty good that at least some of the filenames would be the same. MongoDB cannot assume that identical filenames (even those with identical sizes) are in fact the same file. Thus, there are many cases where it would be a mistake for MongoDB to update the file. Of course, you can use the _id key to update a specific file; and you'll learn more about this topic in the upcoming Python-based experiments.

Determining a File's Length

The put command also returns a file's length, which is both useful information and critical to how GridFS works. While it is nice to know how big a file is for reference, the file's size also plays a big part when you write your own applications. For example, when sending a file over the Web (through HTTP, for example), you need to specify how big the file is. Not all servers do this; for example, when downloading files from certain sites, you may have noticed that your browser can tell you the speed you're downloading the file at, but not how long it will take to finish downloading the file. This is because the server did not provide size information.

Knowing the size of your file is important in one other respect. Earlier, we mentioned that a file is broken up into *chunks*—that is, the file is split into smaller pieces. By default, the chunk size is 256K, but that can be changed to another value if you wish. To work out how many chunks a file takes up, you need to know two things. First you must know how big each chunk is; and second, you must know the file size, so that you can tell how many chunks there are.

You might think that this shouldn't be important. After all, if you have a 1MB file and the chunk size is 256K, then you know that you must start with chunk number four if you want to access data starting at the 800K mark. Yet you still need to know how big the overall file is for the following reason: if you don't know the size, you cannot work out how many valid chunks there are. In the previous example, there's nothing to stop you asking for data that starts at 1.26MB (that is, the sixth chunk). In this case, that chunk doesn't exist, but there is no way to know that without a reference to the file size. Of course, the driver handles all of this for you, so there's no need to worry too much about it; however, knowing how GridFS works "behind the scenes" will certainly help when it comes to debugging your applications.

Working with Chunk Sizes

The put command also returns the chunk size because, although there is a default chunk size, this default can be changed on a file-by-file basis. This allows flexible sizing. If your website streams video, you might want to have many chunks so that you can easily skip to any part of a given video with ease. If you had one big file, you would have to return the whole file, and then find the starting point for the specified section in it. With GridFS, you can pull back data at the chunk level. If you're using the default size, then you can start retrieving data from any 256K chunk. Of course, you can also specify the bit of data you actually want (for example, you might want only five minutes in the middle of a sixty-minute movie). This is a very efficient system, and 256K is a pretty good chunk size for most purposes. If you decide to change it, you should have a good reason for doing so. As always, don't forget to benchmark and test the performance of your custom chunk size; it's not uncommon for theoretically better systems to fail to live up to expectations.

■ **Note**   MongoDB has a 16MB restriction on document size. Because GridFS is simply a different way of storing files in the standard MongoDB framework, this restriction also exists in GridFS. That is, you can't create chunks larger than 16MB. This shouldn't pose a problem, because the whole point of GridFS is to alleviate the need for huge document sizes. If you're worried that you're storing huge files, and this will give you too many chunk documents, you needn't worry—there are MongoDB systems in production with significantly more than a billion documents!

Tracking the Upload Date

The uploadDate key does exactly what its name suggests: it stores the date the file was created in MongoDB. This is a good time to mention that the files collection is just a normal MongoDB collection, containing normal documents. This means that you can add any additional key and value pairs that you need, in the same way you would for any other collection.

For example, consider the case of a real-world application that needs to store text content that you extract from various files. You might need to do this so you could perform some additional indexing and searching. To accomplish this, you might add a file_text key and store the text in there. The elegance of the GridFS system means that you can do anything with this system you can do with any other MongoDB documents. Elegance and power are two of the defining characteristics of working in MongoDB.

Hashing Your Files

MongoDB ships with the MD5 hashing algorithm. You may have come across the algorithm previously when downloading software over the Internet. The theory behind MD5 is that each file has a unique signature. Changing a single bit anywhere in that file will drastically (and noticeably) change the signature. This signature is used for two reasons: security and integrity. For security, if you know what the MD5 hash is supposed to be and you trust the source (perhaps a friend gave it to you), then you can be assured that the file has not been altered if the hash (often called the *checksum*) is correct. This also ensures that the file integrity has been maintained and that no data has been lost or damaged. The MD5 hash of a particular file acts like a fingerprint for a file. The hash can be also used to identify files that have different filenames but have the same contents.

■ **Warning**   The MD5 algorithm is no longer considered secure, and it has been demonstrated that it is possible to create two different files that have the same MD5 checksum, even though their contents are different. In cryptographic terms, this is called a *collision*. Such collisions are bad because they mean it is possible for an attacker to alter a file in such a way that it cannot be detected. This caveat remains somewhat theoretical because a great deal of effort and time would be required to create such collisions intentionally; and even then, the files could be so different as to be obviously not the same file. For this reason, MD5 is still the preferred method of determining file integrity because it is so widely supported. However, if you want to use hashing for its security benefits, you are much better off using one of the SHA family specifications—ideally SHA-256 or SHA-512. Even these hashing families have some theoretical vulnerabilities; however, no one has yet demonstrated a practical case of creating intentional collisions for the SHA family of hashes. MongoDB uses MD5 to ensure file integrity, which is fine for most purposes. However, if you want to hash important data (such as user passwords), you should probably consider using the SHA family of hashes instead.

Looking Under MongoDB's Hood

At this point, you have some data in a MongoDB database. Now let's take a closer look at that data under the covers. To do this, you'll again use some command-line tools to connect to the database and query it. For example, try running the find() command against the file created earlier:

```
$ mongo test
MongoDB shell version: 2.6.5
connecting to: test
```

```
> db.fs.files.find()
{ "_id" : ObjectId("51cb61b26487b3d8ce7af440"), "filename" : "/tmp/
dictionary", "chunkSize" : 262144, "uploadDate" : ISODate("2013-06-
26T21:48:34.621Z"), "md5" : "40c0825855792bd20e8a2d515fe9c3e3", "length" :
4953699 }
>
```

The output should look familiar—after all, it's the same data that you saw earlier in this chapter. Now you can see that the information printed by mongofiles was taken from the file's entry in the fs.files collection.

Next, let's take a look at the chunks collection (we have to add a filter; otherwise, it will show us all of the raw binary data as well):

```
$ mongo test
MongoDB shell version: 2.6.5
connecting to: test
> db.fs.chunks.find({},{"data":0});
{ "_id" : ObjectId("51cb61b29b2daad9857ca205"), "files_id" :
ObjectId("51cb61b26487b3d8ce7af440"), "n" : 4 }
{ "_id" : ObjectId("51cb61b29b2daad9857ca206"), "files_id" :
ObjectId("51cb61b26487b3d8ce7af440"), "n" : 5 }
{ "_id" : ObjectId("51cb61b29b2daad9857ca207"), "files_id" :
ObjectId("51cb61b26487b3d8ce7af440"), "n" : 6 }
{ "_id" : ObjectId("51cb61b29b2daad9857ca208"), "files_id" :
ObjectId("51cb61b26487b3d8ce7af440"), "n" : 7 }
{ "_id" : ObjectId("51cb61b29b2daad9857ca209"), "files_id" :
ObjectId("51cb61b26487b3d8ce7af440"), "n" : 8 }
{ "_id" : ObjectId("51cb61b29b2daad9857ca20a"), "files_id" :
ObjectId("51cb61b26487b3d8ce7af440"), "n" : 9 }
{ "_id" : ObjectId("51cb61b29b2daad9857ca20b"), "files_id" :
ObjectId("51cb61b26487b3d8ce7af440"), "n" : 10 }
{ "_id" : ObjectId("51cb61b29b2daad9857ca20c"), "files_id" :
ObjectId("51cb61b26487b3d8ce7af440"), "n" : 11 }
{ "_id" : ObjectId("51cb61b29b2daad9857ca20d"), "files_id" :
ObjectId("51cb61b26487b3d8ce7af440"), "n" : 12 }
{ "_id" : ObjectId("51cb61b29b2daad9857ca20e"), "files_id" :
ObjectId("51cb61b26487b3d8ce7af440"), "n" : 13 }
{ "_id" : ObjectId("51cb61b29b2daad9857ca20f"), "files_id" :
ObjectId("51cb61b26487b3d8ce7af440"), "n" : 14 }
{ "_id" : ObjectId("51cb61b29b2daad9857ca210"), "files_id" :
ObjectId("51cb61b26487b3d8ce7af440"), "n" : 15 }
{ "_id" : ObjectId("51cb61b29b2daad9857ca211"), "files_id" :
ObjectId("51cb61b26487b3d8ce7af440"), "n" : 16 }
{ "_id" : ObjectId("51cb61b29b2daad9857ca212"), "files_id" :
ObjectId("51cb61b26487b3d8ce7af440"), "n" : 17 }
{ "_id" : ObjectId("51cb61b29b2daad9857ca201"), "files_id" :
ObjectId("51cb61b26487b3d8ce7af440"), "n" : 0 }
{ "_id" : ObjectId("51cb61b29b2daad9857ca202"), "files_id" :
ObjectId("51cb61b26487b3d8ce7af440"), "n" : 1 }
{ "_id" : ObjectId("51cb61b29b2daad9857ca203"), "files_id" :
ObjectId("51cb61b26487b3d8ce7af440"), "n" : 2 }
{ "_id" : ObjectId("51cb61b29b2daad9857ca204"), "files_id" :
ObjectId("51cb61b26487b3d8ce7af440"), "n" : 3 }
{ "_id" : ObjectId("51cb61b29b2daad9857ca213"), "files_id" :
ObjectId("51cb61b26487b3d8ce7af440"), "n" : 18 }>
```

You might wonder why the output here has so many entries. As noted previously, GridFS is just a specification. That is, it uses what MongoDB already provides. While we were testing the commands for the book, the dictionary file was added a couple of times. Later, this file was deleted when we emptied the `fs.files` collection. You can see for yourself what happened next! The fact that some documents were removed from a collection has no bearing on what happens in another collection. Remember: MongoDB doesn't treat these documents or collections in any special way. If the file had been deleted properly through a driver or the `mongofiles` tool, that tool would also have cleaned up the chunks collection.

▓ **Warning** Accessing documents and collections directly is a powerful feature, but you need to be careful. This feature also makes it much easier to shoot yourself in both feet at the same time. Make sure you know what you're doing and that you perform a great deal of testing if you decide to edit these documents and collections manually. Also, keep in mind that the GridFS support in MongoDB's drivers won't know anything about any customizations that you've made.

Using the search Command

Next, let's take a closer look at MongoDB's `search` command. Thus far, there is only a single file in the database, which greatly limits the types of searches you might conduct! So let's add something else. The following snippet copies the dictionary to another file, and then imports that file:

```
$ cp /tmp/dictionary /tmp/hello_world
$ mongofiles put /tmp/hello_world
connected to: 127.0.0.1
added file: { _id: ObjectId('51cb63d167961ebc919edbd5'), filename: "/tmp/
hello_world", chunkSize: 262144, uploadDate: new Date(1372283858021), md5:
"40c0825855792bd20e8a2d515fe9c3e3", length: 4953699 }done!
root@core2:~# mongofiles list
connected to: 127.0.0.1
/tmp/dictionary     4953699
/tmp/hello_world    4953699
$
```

The first line copies the file, and the second line imports it into MongoDB. As in the earlier example, the `put` command prints out the new document that MongoDB has created. Next, you might run the `mongofiles` command `list` to check that the files were correctly stored. If you do so, you can see that there are now two files in the collection; unsurprisingly, both files have the same size.

The search command works exactly as you would expect. All you need to do is tell mongofiles what you are looking for, and it will try to find it for you, as in this example:

```
$ mongofiles search hello
connected to: 127.0.0.1
/tmp/hello_world    4953699
$ mongofiles search dict
connected to: 127.0.0.1
/tmp/dictionary    4953699
$
```

Again, nothing too exciting happens here. However, there is an important takeaway that's worth noting. MongoDB can be as simple or as complex as you need it to be. The mongofiles tool is only for reference use, and it includes very basic debugging. The good news: MongoDB makes it easy to perform simple searches against your files. The even better news: MongoDB also has your back if you want to write some insanely complicated searches.

Deleting

The mongofiles command delete doesn't require much explanation, but it does deserve a big warning. This command deletes files based on the filename. Thus, if you have more than one file with the same name, this command will delete *all* of them. The following snippet shows how to use the delete command:

```
$ mongofiles delete /tmp/hello_world
connected to: 127.0.0.1
$ mongofiles list
connected to: 127.0.0.1
/tmp/dictionary 4953699
$
```

■ **Note**   Many people have commented in connection with this issue that deleting multiple files with the same name is not a problem because no application would have duplicate names. This is simply not true; and in many cases, it doesn't even make sense to enforce unique names. For example, if your app lets users upload photos to their profiles, there's a good chance that half the files you receive will be called photo.jpg or me.png.

Of course, if you are unlikely to use mongofiles to manage your live data—and in truth no one ever expected it to be used that way—then you just need to be careful when deleting data in general.

Retrieving Files from MongoDB

So far, you haven't actually pulled any files out from MongoDB. The most important feature of any database is that it lets you find and retrieve data once it's been put in. The following snippet retrieves a file from MongoDB using the mongofiles command get:

```
$ mongofiles get /tmp/dictionary
connected to: 127.0.0.1
done write to: /tmp/dictionary
$
```

This example includes an intentional mistake. Because it specifies the full name and path of the file you want to retrieve (as required), mongofiles writes the data to a file with the same name and path. Effectively, this overwrites the original dictionary file! This isn't exactly a great loss, because it is being overwritten by the same file—and the dictionary file was only a temporary copy in the first place. Nevertheless, this behavior could give you a rather nasty shock if you accidentally erase two weeks of work. Trust us, you won't figure out where all your work went until sometime after the event! As when using the delete command, you need to be careful when using the get command.

Summing Up mongofiles

The mongofiles utility is a useful tool for quickly looking at what's in your database. If you've written some software, and you suspect something might be amiss with it, then you can use mongofiles to double-check what's going on.

It's an extremely simple implementation, so it doesn't require any fancy logic that could complicate accomplishing the task at hand. Whether you would use mongofiles in a production environment is a matter of personal taste. It's not exactly a Swiss army knife; however, it does provide a useful set of commands that you'll be grateful to have if your application begins misbehaving. In short, you should be familiar with this tool because someday it might be exactly the tool you require to solve an otherwise nettlesome problem.

Exploiting the Power of Python

At this point, you have a solid idea of how GridFS works. Next, you will learn how to access GridFS from Python. Chapter 2 covered how to install PyMongo; if you have any trouble with the examples, please refer back to Chapter 2 and make sure everything is installed correctly.

If you've been following along with the previous examples in this chapter, you should now have one file in GridFS. You'll also recall that the file is a dictionary file, so it contains a list of words. In this section, you will learn how to write a simple Python script that prints out all the words in the dictionary file. Sure, it would be simpler and more efficient to simply cat the original file—but where would the fun be in that?

Begin by firing up Python:

```
Python 2.6.6 (r266:84292, Oct 12 2012, 14:23:48)
[GCC 4.4.6 20120305 (Red Hat 4.4.6-4)] on linux2
Type "help", "copyright", "credits" or "license" for more information.>>>
```

The standard driver for Python is called PyMongo, and it was written by Mike Dirolf. Because the PyMongo driver is supported directly by MongoDB, Inc., the company that publishes MongoDB, you can rest assured that it will be regularly updated and maintained. So, let's go ahead and import the library. You should see something like the following:

```
>>> from pymongo import Connection
>>> import gridfs
>>>
```

If PyMongo isn't installed correctly, you will get an error similar to this:

```
>>> import gridfs
Traceback (most recent call last):
  File "<stdin>", line 1, in <module>
ImportError: No module named gridfs
>>>
```

If you see the latter message, chances are something was missed during installation. In that case, pop back to Chapter 2 and follow the instructions to install PyMongo again.

Connecting to the Database

Before you can retrieve information from a database, you must first establish a connection to it. When you were using the mongofiles utility earlier in this chapter, you probably noticed the reference to 127.0.0.1. This value is also known as the *localhost,* and it represents your computer's loopback address. This value is simply a shortcut for telling a computer to talk to itself. The reason mongofiles mentioned this IP address is that it was actually connecting to MongoDB through the network. The default is to connect to the local machine on the default MongoDB port. Because you haven't changed the default settings, mongofiles can find and connect to your database without any trouble.

When using MongoDB with Python, however, you need to connect to the database and then set up GridFS. Fortunately, this is easy to do:

```
>>> db = Connection().test
>>> fs = gridfs.GridFS(db)
>>>
```

The first line opens the connection and selects the database. By default, mongofiles uses the test database; hence, you'll find your dictionary file in test. The second line sets up GridFS and prepares it for use.

Accessing the Words

In its original implementation, the PyMongo driver used a file-like interface to leverage GridFS. This is somewhat different from what you saw in this chapter's earlier examples with mongofiles, which were more FTP-like in nature. In the original implementation of PyMongo, you could read and write data just as you do for a normal file.

This made PyMongo very much like Python to use, and it allowed for easy integration with existing scripts. However, this behavior was changed in version 1.6 of the driver, and this functionality is no longer supported. While very Python-like, the behavior had some problems that made the tool less effective overall.

Generally speaking, the PyMongo driver attempts to make GridFS files look and feel like ordinary files on the filesystem. On the one hand, this is nice because it means there's no learning curve, and the driver is usable with any method that requires a file. On the other hand, this approach is somewhat limiting and doesn't give a good feel for how powerful GridFS is. Important changes were made to how PyMongo works in version 1.6, particularly in how get and put work.

■ **Note** This revised version of PyMongo isn't too dissimilar from previous versions of the tool, and many people who used the previous API have found it easy to adapt to the revised version. That said, Mike's changes haven't gone down well with everybody. For example, some people found the file-based keying in the old API to be extremely useful and easy to use. The revised version of PyMongo supports the ability to create filenames, so the missing behavior can be replicated in the revised version; however, doing so does require a bit more code.

Putting Files into MongoDB

Getting files into GridFS through PyMongo is straightforward and intentionally similar to the way you do so using command-line tools. MongoDB is all about throughput, and the changes to the API in the revised version of PyMongo reflect this. Not only do you get better performance, but the changes also bring the Python driver in line with the other GridFS implementations.

Let's put the dictionary into GridFS (again):

```
>>> with open("/tmp/dictionary") as dictionary:
...     uid = fs.put(dictionary)
...
>>> uid
ObjectId('51cb65be2f50332093f67b98') >>>
```

In this example, you use the put method to insert the file. It's important that you capture the result from this method because it contains the document _id for your file. PyMongo takes a different approach than mongofiles, which assumes the filename is effectively the key (even though you can have duplicates). Instead, PyMongo references files based on their _id. If you don't capture this information, then you won't be able to reliably find the file again. Actually, that's not strictly true—you could *search* for a file quite easily—but if you want to link this file to a particular user account, then you need this _id.

Two useful arguments that can be used in conjunction with the put command are filename and content_type. As you might expect, these arguments let you set the filename and the content type of the file, respectively. This is useful for loading files directly from disk. However, it is even handier when you're handling files that have been received over the Internet or generated in memory because, in those cases, you can use file-like semantics, but without actually having to create a real file on the disk.

Retrieving Files from GridFS

At long last, you're now ready to return your data! At this point, you have your unique _id, so finding the file is easy. The get method retrieves a file from GridFS:

```
>>> new_dictionary = fs.get(uid)
```

That's it! The preceding snippet returns a file-like object; thus, you can print all the words in the dictionary using the following snippet:

```
>>> for word in new_dictionary:
...     print word
```

Now watch in awe as a list of words quickly scrolls up the screen! Okay, so this isn't exactly rocket science. However, the fact that it isn't rocket science or in any way difficult is part of the beauty of GridFS—it does work as advertised, and it does so in an intuitive and easily understood way!

Deleting Files

Deleting a file is also easy. All you have to do is call fs.delete() and pass the _id of the file, as in the following example:

```
>>> fs.delete(uid)
>>> new_dictionary = fs.get(uid)
Traceback (most recent call last):
  File "<stdin>", line 1, in <module>
  File "/usr/lib/python2.6/site-packages/pymongo-2.5.2-py2.6-linux-x86_64.
egg/gridfs/__init__.py", line 140, in get
```

```
    return GridOut(self.__collection, file_id)
  File "/usr/lib/python2.6/site-packages/pymongo-2.5.2-py2.6-linux-x86_64.egg/
gridfs/grid_file.py", line 392, in __init__
    (files, file_id))
gridfs.errors.NoFile: no file in gridfs collection Collection(Database(Conne
ction('localhost', 27017), u'test'), u'fs.files') with _id ObjectId('51cb65b
e2f50332093f67b98') >>>
```

These results could look a bit scary, but they are just PyMongo's way of saying that it couldn't find the file. This isn't surprising, because you just deleted it!

Summary

In this chapter, you undertook a fast-paced tour of GridFS. You learned what GridFS is, how it fits together with MongoDB, and how to use its basic syntax. This chapter didn't explore GridFS in great depth, but in the next chapter, you'll learn how to integrate GridFS with a real application using PHP. For now, it's enough to understand how GridFS can save you time and hassle when storing files and other large pieces of data.

In the next chapter, you'll start putting what you've learned to real use—specifically, you'll learn how to build a fully functional address book!

Index

Get the eBook for only $10!

> Now you can take the weightless companion with you anywhere, anytime. Your purchase of this book entitles you to 3 electronic versions for only $10.

This Apress title will prove so indispensible that you'll want to carry it with you everywhere, which is why we are offering the eBook in 3 formats for only $10 if you have already purchased the print book.

Convenient and fully searchable, the PDF version enables you to easily find and copy code—or perform examples by quickly toggling between instructions and   applications. The MOBI format is ideal for your Kindle, while the ePUB can be utilized on a variety of mobile devices.

Go to www.apress.com/promo/tendollars to purchase your companion eBook.

CPSIA information can be obtained at www.ICGtesting.com
Printed in the USA
LVOW07s0501301214

420874LV00001BA/109/P